T0294649

The Project Management Handbook

A Guide to Capital Improvements

Kevin P. Vida

GOVERNMENT INSTITUTES
An imprint of
THE SCARECROW PRESS, INC.
Lanham • Toronto • Plymouth, UK
2012

 **Government Institutes**

Published by Government Institutes
An imprint of The Scarecrow Press, Inc.
A wholly owned subsidiary of The Rowman & Littlefield Publishing Group, Inc.
4501 Forbes Boulevard, Suite 200, Lanham, Maryland 20706
www.rowman.com

10 Thornbury Road, Plymouth PL6 7PP, United Kingdom

British Library Cataloguing in Publication Information Available

Library of Congress Cataloging-in-Publication Data

Vida, Kevin P., 1968-
The project management handbook : a guide to capital improvements / Kevin P. Vida.
    p. cm.
  Includes bibliographical references and index.
  ISBN 978-1-60590-788-8 (cloth : alk. paper) — ISBN 978-1-60590-789-5 (ebook)
  1. Project management. 2. Capital budget. I. Title.
HD69.P75V5293 2012

                                          658.4'04—dc232012016628

∞™ The paper used in this publication meets the minimum requirements of American National Standard for Information Sciences—Permanence of Paper for Printed Library Materials, ANSI/NISO Z39.48-1992.

Printed in the United States of America

Contents

Preface

The Project Management Handbook has been developed as a basic text for providing a baseline of phases, tasks, strategies, and tips related to project management philosophies for students, government officials, construction and project managers (CMs/PMs), and executives who want a detailed look at what PMs do in order to achieve project success.

This book will also be helpful to those training or apprenticing in the architecture, engineering, and construction industry (AEC), along with students, business managers, project managers, and construction managers.

It is important to note that not all the philosophies utilized in the general practice of project management are demonstrated here, due to the nature of this specific type of project management. It is recommended that users of this book gain basic knowledge of project management practices so that they can understand how this book integrates certain project management practices while not using others.

In preparing this text I have used my many years of experience to develop a clear and concise combination of phases, stages, tasks, and strategies for a proven and technically correct book.

The book can be used in many ways. It is ideal for anyone involved in AEC or management as it relates to capital improvement programs. It can serve as a supplement or a stand-alone to many courses of instruction. Readers who follow the instructions provided will be able to do the following:

- Gain general knowledge about project management.
- Identify stakeholders/users involved throughout a project.
- Gain knowledge of how a project progresses from inception through completion.

- Develop documents, such as contracts, to execute projects.
- Learn how different entities interact with a project.
- Process documents related to design and construction.
- Implement processes using project management tools.
- Display competency in tracking project progress.
- Develop an after-action report that includes a comparison of the original goals and the actual achievements along with lessons learned.

Acknowledgments

I would like to start by thanking my wonderful wife, Shawna, along with my daughters, Jessica and Madison, my mother, and my father, for without their encouragement and support this book would not exist. Additionally, I would like to thank the University of Michigan-Architecture, Engineering, and Construction (UM-AEC) for the use and reproduction of certain materials included in this book. Finally, my thanks to the Engineers Joint Contract Documents Committee (EJCDC) for allowing me to use and reproduce their documents as samples. The committee's knowledge and continued support in the field of engineering and construction is greatly appreciated.

Introduction

Very few project managers (PMs) operating under the auspice of a capital improvement program (CIP) have any formal technical training or education in project management. In my case, architectural engineering technology was my field of choice, and most of my technical training, education, and experiences are derived from the architecture, engineering, and construction industry.

While most of my project management skills were developed as a result of on-the-job training, mentors, and personal experiences, the learning curve was steep. Help from my office chief to develop an understanding of how the organization expects their CIP to be managed and executed was both timely and costly. It involved a year of on-the-job training before acquiring an understanding of my organization's operational procedures and meeting the different divisional counterparts that I would be interacting with on projects.

As with many engineers and architects who find themselves working as a project manager, and given the multitude of different ways an organization is set up to operate, it would have been beneficial to have a baseline system of universal tasks to navigate all the different levels of bureaucracy efficiently in order to successfully complete a project on time and within budget.

I developed this book to do just that, by providing a general, practical, easy-to-understand way of how a project is developed, executed, monitored, and completed. For simplification, I divided the chapters into phases, and then progressive tasks, and steps, so my advice is to start at the beginning to develop an understanding of the project life cycle.

Project managers are used throughout different industries; you'll find them in computer services, architecture and engineering fields, local, state, and federal governments, and the private sector.

To be a project manager, excellent people skills are a must, along with the ability to welcome and accept criticism. If you like a fast-paced, challenging career in a high-stress environment, and like serving others, then this career is a perfect fit for you. The variety of tasks required on a daily basis may have a PM developing design contracts, reviewing documents, processing a change order, interviewing/evaluating firms, developing in-house operational procedures, or attending construction progress meetings, to name a few.

I compare a project manager to a professional quarterback, in that you need to have an excellent understanding of the rules; have a good playbook, which I'm providing here; react quickly to changing conditions; know your strengths and weaknesses; identify and mitigate risks; be accurate; and most of all, learn from your mistakes. You will make mistakes, and how big they are is determined by how well you prepared for contingencies during the planning stage. Remember that if anything can go wrong, it will.

Transparency is a must in this profession. If a person in the chain of command asks an unknown question, resist the urge to guess; if you guess wrong, the entire office will gain an atmosphere of distrust. It is completely fine to say that you are not sure and will get back to them with the right answer in a timely manner after you have gathered your thoughts and facts. It is hard to admit that we are not perfect at what we do, but honesty is always the best policy. In time, this will help your organization gain trust in your ability and skills.

I once heard it said that "if quarterbacks do not throw an interception now and then, they are just not trying hard enough." That definitely applies to project managers. At some point you will be asked to make a decision that has the potential of being wrong, but not making a decision could end up costing the organization more in the end. Minimizing risk with proper planning will help you make a more logical and balanced decision. Expect that some mistakes will be made, but don't waste the experience; learn from it. Document it in the final project report so that others in your office can also learn from it.

Project managers seem to be more comfortable among chaos while maintaining a level of professionalism that keeps projects on track. Being a good PM is about projects being completed on time and within budget, so having some thick skin is required. Remember, you are charged with being a good steward of your organization's money, so being firm but respectful are necessary traits and half the battle to successfully completing a project.

WHAT TO EXPECT

Because I am employed as a project manager in county government, with extensive experience in vertical construction and road projects, I will be discussing tasks in the following chapters in technical terms related to these fields.

After reading this book, you will know what steps are required, along with the roles and responsibilities a project manager has in executing a CIP project successfully. Be it a building, road, bridge, or utility construction project, you will acquire the skills and ability to navigate through the processes involved in executing a project as required and outlined in an approved CIP.

1

Project Management Basics

SOQ, RFQ (with two meanings), IDQ, RFB, CIP, RFP, QBS, RFI, CCD, COs, PCOs, JIT, SOP, IFB, ITB. What do these acronyms mean? In project management they all have a specific meaning and use. In this book we will describe them as they apply to the project management life cycle.

PROJECT LIFE CYCLE

A project, as defined in *A Guide to the Project Management Body of Knowledge (PMBOK Guide),*[1] is "a temporary endeavor undertaken to create a unique product, service, or result." When this definition is applied to a product life cycle that in the end results in a product meeting all objectives, you can deduce that every project has a beginning and an end with many tasks in the middle. When this definition is applied to a project life cycle, which is a collection of activities/tasks, processes, stages, or phases, these activities combine to produce the successful output of a completed project. Within the required parameters of cost and time, you can develop a project management plan, along with a project charter with work authorization provided through a work authorization system, allowing the work of a project to take you from project start-up through completion.

Typically the basic schedule activities/tasks and phases for capital improvement programs (CIPs) seem to stay the same from project to project. The exception to the rule is when a building project does not require designs or drawings, but rather a scope of work described under a request for quote (RFQ) based on a performance type specification with minimum permit requirements.

5

Since projects are temporary and have defined starting and end points as outputs, project costs differ from overall product life cycle costs that are considered ongoing operational costs. The product life cycle continues on when the project life cycle ends. It includes the costs of final product/deliverable operation and maintenance that will be performed routinely and as needed to keep the product operational.

WHAT IS PROJECT MANAGEMENT?

According to *A Guide to PMBOK*,[2] project management (PM) is the application of knowledge, skills, tools, and techniques to project activities to meet project requirements. Projects are typically smaller than the organization, which may have several projects waiting for assignment under a program developed by program management or the project management office (PMO). So managing a project first requires that a product or service be conceived by way of showing a need for the product, and then approved by the organization via the project charter, before processes, project management groups, or process groups are initiated. Once approved, a project manager, who may hold a credential as a project management professional (PMP®) through the Project Management Institute's (PMI®) certification program, or an entire project team will be assigned to start the initiating process based on the constraints of time, money, and scope/quality. These constraints can be affected depending on the desired requirements of the organization. Referred to as the triple constraint,[3] it is a visual representation depicting how competing demands affect each other. For instance, you may have proper amounts of time and scope allotted but it will end up costing more for quality. In order to bring the cost down you may end up balancing this triangle by sacrificing quality. Risks related to unforeseen conditions can also affect this triangle. So project managers (PMs) need to be aware of and take preventative action or risk avoidance via risk response planning and risk mitigation techniques. The key is to balance all three constraints by benchmarking and noting any positive or negative effects throughout the overall project. By performing a probability and impact matrix and a sensitivity analysis and then developing a risk management plan, including any previously identified risks from other similar projects documented in a risk database that includes a risk identification process and a risk breakdown structure tailored specifically for an individual project, along with PMO risk categories, a PM can then perform a qualitative and quantitative risk analysis and a strengths, weaknesses, opportunities, and threats analysis (SWOT) to avoid a rework or perform a workaround of the project requirements. Be aware that taking these actions may cause a residual and secondary risk event.

Most projects have five project phases or groups, also called project management process groups, from beginning to end. According to *A Guide to PMBOK*,[4] they are as follows:

1. Project initiation stage: This phase includes confirmation that a project baseline has been approved and a project manager assigned to develop a project outline. According to the *Project Management Professional Study Guide*[5] the following elements make up a project outline:
   - Project overview
   - Goals and objectives
   - Schedule of deliverables
   - Need for the project
   - Product scope description
   - Resources and cost estimates
   - Feasibility study results
   - Staffing requirements and subject matter experts (SMEs)
   - Roles and responsibilities of the team members

   Based on the answers related to its application area, the relevant elements and the voice of the customer, the project manager (PM) begins the development of a project scope management plan, project scope statement, product scope, product scope descriptions, planning packages, project schedule network plan/network logic, work breakdown structure (WBS), work breakdown structure components, activity attributes, activity codes, activity descriptions, performance measurement baselines, and a statement of qualifications (SOQ) followed by a request for proposal (RFP) that will include all the project elements required to develop and design project documents. Once a design firm wins a bid, based on the firm's score, a contract for required services is executed and planning can take place. If the project is related to construction where design and construction is required, the phases required are as follows:

2. Project planning and design stage: This is made up of elements that will generate a product for construction. In my organization we use planning to develop project documents for bidding on the construction of a product; in my case it is usually a facility.

3. Project execution and construction stage: Once all the plans have been developed and approved and ready for advertisement, the procurement process for construction-related services is started and a contract awarded.

4. Project monitoring and controlling during construction: After contracts are finalized and agreements signed, the work begins and the organization monitors the construction of the product, ensuring that it is being built in accordance with the directions (plans and specifications/project manual).

The project manager, construction manager, and engineer will oversee the production and schedule so that the project is completed on time and within budget.

5. Project Closing (use and occupancy): Once the contractor's work is complete and accepted by the organization for use or sale, the PM provides all the required information needed for the operational life cycle to start, and develops and submits a final record document that summarizes the project's performance and any lessons learned throughout the project's phases.

WHAT IS A CAPITAL IMPROVEMENT PROGRAM (CIP)?

Before we get into the nuts and bolts of executing a successful project, we need a brief introduction describing the essence of a CIP. Since there are many books already written on this subject, I will spare you an in-depth description.

According to the Massachusetts Department of Revenue,[6] a CIP is based on a comprehensive plan developed to meet an organization's anticipated growth and expansion. It is a document that organizes projects in a well-thought-out plan to produce, preserve, or enhance a product and/or service. A CIP acts as a pathway between the comprehensive plan and allocation of funds to be spent on a project. As part of the evaluation, a four- to six-year outlook is developed based on identified needs that will require funds for building projects that support operations. Composed of two parts—the capital budget, which forecasts short range plans, and capital program, which forecasts long range plans—it is a snapshot of upcoming expenditures based on the outlook mentioned.

Some of the line items you will find in a government CIP could include equipment, such as vehicles, lawn equipment, heavy equipment, general maintenance/repair items, and sundries. Additionally, these will include new construction or renovation projects for buildings and structures like parks, community centers, libraries, water and wastewater treatment facilities, fire stations, police stations, roads and bridges, courthouses, and more.

BIRTH OF A CIP

When a municipality, private organization, educational institution, or local government determines a need for its organization, it develops a project plan and describes the need in a CIP. A committee made up of key personnel in the organization will participate in the CIP review process with the organization's finance and budget division, considered the subject matter experts, and a diverse mix of people to help ensure that the CIP be developed without favoritism and assigned based on a balanced budget that prioritizes the most urgent needs by reviewing, ranking, and establishing, on an annual basis, the projects to be included in the organization's budget.

Before an organization determines if a project has merit, a request is submitted to the CIP committee for review and inclusion into the overall CIP review process. For example, in government CIP development, projects can be prioritized by need in relation to public health, safety, welfare, operational costs for services, and growth management. In order to keep existing assets functional, requests can be submitted that include major repairs, renovations or replacement of existing assets, or new facilities in order to keep services operating efficiently. For a project to be accepted into the CIP, certain criteria must be met. For instance, your organization may require that each committee person ask the following questions to make sure the project meets their needs:[7]

- Is the project needed in order to implement an ongoing project?
- Is the project in a designated growth area?
- Does it duplicate services?
- Does it reduce operational and energy costs?
- Does it provide enhanced or new services related to public health, safety, welfare, or operational costs for services?
- Is there a need required to meet state/federal laws or court rulings?
- Does the project qualify for any grants?
- Does the project spur private investment in communities and improve the local economy?
- Is there a measurable environmental benefit?
- Do revenue sources support realistic funding sources based on a review of revenue conditions?

Unlike the federal government, states, counties, and municipalities are constitutionally bound to provide a balanced budget by law. To that end, organizations try to identify, prioritize, and develop a strategic plan that will support or enhance services. Using a cost-benefit analysis (CBA) is a way that organizations can evaluate the cost versus the benefits of a project request expressed in monetary values, as described in *Cost-Benefit Analysis and the Environment*.[8] As part of the CBA review, PMs sometimes will use a benefit-cost ratio (BCR) as an indicator to determine if a project is feasible. For example, your organization may see a need to expand their general office space. The cost for construction is estimated at \$4.5 million with a completed value of \$5.0 million. Using the calculation \$5.0 million ÷ \$4.5 million = 1.11 (a positive ratio), this indicates that the project is a viable option.

Since I am not an accountant or a CPA, I suggest further researching documents related to CBA, along with CBA formulas, for an in-depth review.

Many CIPs in local governments eventually have an operational cost component that is tied to the "bricks-and-mortar" money assigned to a project. In some cases, construction and operational money may be available through several sources of funds such as general obligation bonds (GO bonds), impact fees, personal property taxes, recordation taxes, enterprise funds, federal grants, state grants, or other sources such as endowments, trust funds, or donations. In some cases, money for operation or construction of a new project may not be available and vice versa. Financing and issuing bonds can help bridge the gap, because they help spread the cost over a certain number of years and are paid as part of the organization's debt service. Debt service is somewhat like paying a home mortgage in that over a given period, the interest and principal on the debt must be repaid. Organizations typically engage a financial organization that specializes in issuing bonds. They use three rating agencies—Moody's, Standard & Poor's, and Fitch Ratings—that rate your organization's bond status. A rating of triple A (AAA) will give your organization the best interest rate when paying back the debt service. The better the rating, the better the organization's interest rate. An organization with a bond rating below BBB/Baa are labeled as junk status and will have an extremely hard time issuing bonds and getting a good interest rate, thus limiting their ability to provide improvements to their constituency.

After the CIP committee and finance department approve a fully funded CIP, the stakeholders/users can then proceed with their individual projects and will engage the office of project management, or an outside firm that specializes in project management, to execute the project. Some organizations have an in-house PMO.

OTHER PROJECT SELECTION METHODS

Using a CBA method for small projects may not be prudent, since they do not have the same type of scrutiny that a bigger, more elaborate, project may have. In this case, we would use several other methods, in combination or individually, to determine if a project is feasible and provide a go/no-go, or make-or-buy decision.

- Net present value (NPV): Using the NPV method allows an organization to determine a project represented in today's value based on a discounted cash flow while taking into account the initial or sunk cost of the project. For example, NPV equals the amount of discounted cash flows—the project cost and any cost obtained to recycle the final product once it has exhausted its useful life. So before you can determine if a project is feasible, you need to know the present value (PV) of the product and the future value of the product (FV). PV represents the time value of money based on the amount of cash needed for start-up costs and the loan percentage given for a number of years. For instance, a $10.00 investment now at a 10% interest would have a FV of $10.00 $\times$ $(1 + .10)^1 = \$11.00$. Knowing this formula we can apply the following example. Your office needs a new plotter. The cost for the machine and labor to set it up is $50,000.00. The organization would need to obtain a loan to buy the plotter; the bank sets the loan rate at 10% and the useful life of the plotter is four years. Additionally, plotting prints in-house saves the organization $15,000.00 a year. Based on the formula $(FV) = PV (1 + interest)^n$, and table 1.1, the plotter project is showing a positive cost thus indicating that the project is feasible.
- Internal rate of return (IRR): Not used very much in project management, IRR is a complicated formula and better left to the CPAs. Keep in mind that IRR is used when choosing between projects that have an NPV of zero. The project with the best, that is, higher IRR should be the winner of the two project options.
- Opportunity cost: Consider for a moment that you can only invest project dollars toward one project at a time. A project comes along that provides a profit of $10,000.00. But in the future, you can do a project that produces the product differently while staying within the statement of work (SOW) and provides a profit of $15,000.00. By passing on the first opportunity you have increased your profit by $5,000.00. The $5,000.00 represents the risk of making more money based on a potentially great opportunity.
- Payback period: This represents the amount of time required to make back your investment. The goal is to recoup your sunk costs sooner as opposed to later.
- Return on investment (ROI): This represents the amount of money you make from investing in something. For example, using the NPV example, you decide to buy the plotter for $50,000.00; this is the investment cost. By doing the project your company can save $60,000.00 over 4 years. Using the ROI formula which is (savings − investment) ÷ investment, then the ROI = ($60,000 − $50,000) ÷ $50,000 = 20%. Keep in mind that the bigger the ROI the better. A negative ROI indicates that the project should not be accepted.

Table 1.1

Year	FV (savings, i.e., inflows)	PV
0 = investment cost	(-$50,000.00)	(-$50,000.00)
1 $(1 + .10)^1 = 1.1000$	$15,000.00 ÷ 1.1000	$13,636.36
2 $(1 + .10)^2 = 1.2100$	$15,000.00 ÷ 1.2100	$12,396.94
3 $(1 + .10)^3 = 1.3310$	$15,000.00 ÷ 1.3310	$11,269.72
4 $(1 + .10)^4 = 1.4641$	$15,000.00 ÷ 1.4641	$10,245.20
Recycled profit		$9,000.00
Total NPV		$6,548.22

THE PROJECT MANAGEMENT OFFICE (PMO)

As a performing organization, project management offices, which contain a war room and/or have virtual team capabilities, can be described as three types: functional, matrix, or projectized.[9] A functional organization, with a functional manager, provides PMs little or no authority. Matrix organizations provide PMs moderate to high authoritative levels; this is how my office is described. Finally, projectized organizations offer PMs the most authority regarding resources, project budget, and administrative staff. The office of project management in an organization such as a county government might consist of a department head, office chief, and the project managers. The hierarchy of passing down a project starts with the CIP committee who directs a program department head who then directs the performing organization's office chief to assign approved projects to a PM.

After the office chief assigns a project to a PM, the wheels of project management start moving. At this point you're directed to take the ball and start the process of implementing the project plan. But before we get too far ahead of ourselves, let's identify what information the office chief may provide to get us started (see figure 1.1).

THE PROJECT MANAGER'S HAND TOOLS

Most of the work you will perform as a PM will require interacting with people associated with the projects assigned to you, and it is in the users' and your best interest to see that you succeed. Therefore, your verbal and written communication skills must be excellent. You must be able to clearly express your thoughts and recommendations in a manner that allows your users to

<u>*Sample Project (information provided by an adopted CIP)*</u>

Project Name: Anytown Fire Company #1 Fire Station

Description/Justification of project:
    The Anytown Fire Company #1, which is part of Hometown Volunteer Fire Company, is located at 123 main street, hometown, USA and owned by the Hometown Volunteer Fire Company. A new station is being proposed to be built on ground owned by the Fire Company located at 2nd. Street. The current building, which was built in 1887, is too small for the current needs of the Fire Company. This project would build a new 5 bay station and administrative areas in accordance with the previously developed fire station program developed and used for all fire stations. The company is requesting 17,000 square feet for the fire station.

Capacity: 5 Firefighters on duty 24 hrs a day

Project costs (in Thousands):
Architecture and Engineering (425.00)
Site Improvements (200.50)
Construction (4,200.00)
Inspection (200.50)
Equipment (150.00)
IIT Equipment (90.50)
Project Management (70.50)

Total Cost: 5,337.00

In addition to the information in figure 1.1 your office chief explains that you will need to work with the users and the purchasing department to develop an advertisement for an architect that will provide design services related to the fire stations construction. We will get into those details in a later chapter.

Figure 1.1

make better decisions and keep projects moving along the product cycle path. For instance, you may be interested in obtaining review comments or recommendations from users before moving on to the next task, but because they are not the primary user in the project and have more immediate priorities, they may see your request as not rising to the same level of urgency. This is when you need to implement your communication skills in a savvy and tactful way that will motivate these users to respond in a timely manner, thus keeping your project on track. In order to do that, you will need to use some communication tools.

In addition to traditional office supplies, including but not limited to a digital camera (10 megapixel minimum), flash drive (4 GB minimum), calculators, color scanners, color copiers, tape measuring instruments, laser pointer, rulers, architectural and engineering scales, along with plenty of post-it notes and red pens, there are some key tools that I have found helpful when expediting a project successfully.

- Computer: This is obvious but important for developing documents and communicating quickly through e-mail and other types of software. Computers make communication, budget tracking, document development, and record keeping a snap. Keeping track of all the information generated throughout a project can become critical throughout the life cycle of a project. At minimum, I recommend using preloaded software, such as e-mail, spreadsheet, and writing software, because some of your team members will most likely have the same software preloaded on their computers, making coordination easy and efficient without having to pay for additional software.
- Project tracking software: Many companies have developed good and practical project management software that can be used to set up a project management system to track project progress. If your organization is not currently using one, I would ask for it or find one that you are comfortable using. It will allow you to update any stakeholders and management quickly, and provide a permanent record of project performance for later review. Some software is all-inclusive, allowing you to produce change orders, payment requisitions, and more. The Internet is a good source to find a variety of proprietary and free project management software.
- Cell phones: I can recall several occasions when a cell phone has saved me a day's worth of work. It allows you to multitask much easier and is necessary in an emergency.

At the end of a project, and for many years after, these tools will have satisfactorily detailed records showing how a project performed overall and will document any lessons learned.

KEY PLAYERS

In every organization there is a chain of command. In this book I have presented the key people that are needed to successfully complete a project based on my experience in county government and in other organizations. Due to current fiscal constraints seen in governments across the county, one or only a handful of people may perform multiple duties. For example, the organization's director of operations may also be the PM, or assume any of the other roles required to successfully achieve a desired result. The government hierarchy has several divisions that specialize in providing different services to support operations throughout the organization. Project managers, though working and networking for the public indirectly, are often working for internal government agencies that provide services directly to the public, such as fire/rescue services, police, libraries, and more. Some divisions outlined may be combined in smaller governments, such as a municipal or town government, but the chain of command ends at the board of county commissioners, an organization's CEO, a county executive, or a mayor and board.

1. Board of County Commissioners (BOCC): There are several different forms of government: home rule, charter, and commissioner. Since I work for a commissioner type of government, this book is developed around a commissioner-based organization made up of, in my case, five commissioners. A project manager may interact with the BOCC when decisions are needed based on county policies and when making recommendations for awarding design contracts through the purchasing department. Approvals are made, based on your recommendation, by collective vote during work sessions and administrative business meetings. It is important to mention that if a question is asked and you do not know the answer, don't guess. Inform them that you are not sure and will research the issue in further detail before responding back in a timely manner.

2. Users/stakeholders/sponsors: In an organization such as county government, there are several divisions: public works, fire/rescue services, and more. The one thing they have in common is that directors are in charge of each division and they all have requests for projects in the CIP. A project manager will network with these divisions when a project is assigned to develop a project scope management plan, project scope statement, and perform a Monte Carlo analysis if needed. The director may be your point of contact, or possibly an assigned representative. It is important to know whom you are working with and if they have been through the project life cycle before, as this will help you later when submitting documents for review. Some users may have an understanding of construction; others may have limited experience identifying problems and translating issues into comments. Keep in mind that changes requested by a user is less costly during design than when requested during construction. So if you take some time in preparing a sketch for new users to review for concurrence, you may be able to provide enough visualization so they can then make an educated decision as to what they want. An example would be using 18-inch deep wall cabinets as opposed to 12-inch cabinets in a kitchenette, because big plates are typically 15 inches in diameter and typically stored in a wall cabinet. Or during design, a user may be fine with the configuration of this kitchenette and then during construction

they would like to add an additional 80 square feet for vending machine space. This would definitely delay the project due to structural evaluations of the floor area proposed and any redesign required in order for the contractor to provide a price for the requested work. In many cases the cost to redesign is not worth the extra cost and extension of contract time. Users may not be aware of the impacts caused by their request.

3. County manager: A county manager is considered the executive that has full responsibility for the day-to-day operations of all county divisions and departments and serves at the pleasure of the board, as do the division directors that serve under this person. Project managers have limited interaction with county managers since your division director, department head, and office chief make up the chain of command.

4. Legal department: Legal personnel help with any legal needs that a project manager may have. They assist in reviewing and approving contract documents, land acquisition, titling, and legal opinions. Some organizations will have a lawyer on retainer or have an in-house legal department.

5. Land acquisition coordinator: This person will perform all required levels of effort to purchase property. This will include deed searches, titles, negotiation of land contracts, and any services required to obtain land.

6. Division director: Depending on how big your organization is, you may have many divisions under the BOCC umbrella. Each division director is responsible for the day-to-day operations of that division. While also serving at the pleasure of the board, division directors are managed by the county manager. In my organization, our office is part of the division of public works. The director also identifies division needs, which are later requested in the proposed overall CIP.

7. Department head: The department head may have several offices to supervise, including the project management office. This person is supervised by the division director and plays an important role in representing the overall department. The head develops and implements policies for day-to-day operational support for the PMO.

8. Office chief/engineering manager: The office chief, sometimes called an engineering manager, is your direct supervisor for day-to-day operations; this person is responsible for staffing all activities performed in the PMO. Based on a staffing management plan and by assigning and prioritizing project requests based on resource planning, resource breakdown structures (RBS), resource-limited schedules, resource calendars, resource histograms, the approved CIP, and organizational needs, the office chief performs resource-leveling techniques to spread projects among project managers. If you encounter a problem on a project or need direction about policies and procedures, the office chief is your first point of

contact. Project updates are routinely provided to the chief for review and distribution throughout the chain of command. The chief also may mentor staff members on projects if a project manager needs help in solving an issue. Additionally, the office chief and other project managers are a good source of knowledge regarding issues. They may have been through the same problem and have recommendations on how to proceed. Working with department heads, directors, and stakeholders, they also develop should-cost estimates and/or three-point estimates for budget recommendations.

9. Finance: When CIP programs are approved, the finance division is the gatekeeper and tracks budget information. Project managers who have a project that needs additional funds will work with finance to adjust and approve a budget via a budget transfer request. Organizations typically set up a threshold of approval; for instance, the finance division may have a policy, approved by the organization, to approve transfer requests up to a certain dollar amount.

10. Management services: A management services division is responsible for maintaining, determining, and providing space allocations for the organization. They track building inventory that includes rental spaces, county-owned buildings, and future buildings. For shell space in existing facilities or new space, they will either obtain new land via a land acquisition coordinator or use county-owned land. A project manager will network with this division or its designated representative during land acquisition and the design phase of a project and will work with the users to develop a project management plan, scope definition, budget, and reserve analysis for any new spaces or furniture that may be required. Furniture, in the eyes of a project manager, is any equipment that is not mechanically fastened or built in. So when developing a scope of services for design it is essential to work with the user and management services to identify and budget equipment from items included in the overall construction budget, such as cabinets or specialty items.

11. Purchasing manager: When developing a Statement of Qualifications (SOQs) (see appendix A), Requests for Proposal (RFPs) (see appendix B), Requests for Quote (RFQ) via an Indefinite Quantity Contract (IDQ) (see appendix C), or recommending an award, a purchasing manager assigned as your point of contract is the gatekeeper for these tasks. You may develop these documents, but purchasing approves and advertises them based on the organization's procurement rules. As with finance, purchasing will also have policies that allow them to approve purchases up to a certain amount before needing to go through a formal bid process. During the advertisement process, the purchasing manager will receive

and track requests for information (RFIs) from prospective bidders and route them to the PM for review and comment. The answers are then sent back to the purchasing manager so that responses can be issued by way of addendum. After bid award, the purchasing manager also gathers all required bonding information, such as bid, payment, and performance bonds (See appendix D).

12. Facility services department (may be a branch of the management services division): Project managers interact with facility services when identifying specific equipment that they have standardized throughout buildings that they service. This is done so that purchasing the same sundries creates value through bulk purchases, also known as buying base on an economy of scale. The facility services department performs housekeeping tasks such as general cleaning and waxing floors. Items that they will specify for design include bathroom trash receptacles, paper towel dispensers, soap dispensers, and other janitorial fixtures.

13. Maintenance (may be a branch of the management services division): Maintenance is very involved throughout design and construction of every project, especially during construction document development, when this department has subprojects being performed concurrently with your project. When developing plans for renovations or new construction, maintenance personnel provide a quality plan and details on standards and guidelines for building systems equipment, which may be found in their total quality management plan (TQM) and can monitor system reliability. These details are provided to the design firm in the form of a maintenance standards checklist and an owner's project requirements (OPR) sheet (see appendix B). This includes, but is not limited to, locks, heating and cooling systems (HVAC), door hardware, and paint—basically any equipment that they will be maintaining. If you are in a small organization, one or two people may be in charge of all the building systems. In a large organization you may have several different maintenance staff who specialize in this field. Below is a list of maintenance staff that may be needed to interact with the project manager when developing specifications for buildings systems:

   • Head maintenance technician: Depending on size, full-time technicians are assigned a facility or facilities and perform all the general upkeep and scheduled routine maintenance; this is operating cost and part of the overall life-cycle cost of a final product until it has maximized its useful life. The technician may also supervise one or two maintenance staff. A project manager will interact with this person when one of the buildings has a CIP project budgeted. For example, a head maintenance technician servicing a facility, along with the director of maintenance, identifies a need to replace some HVAC units. After maintenance describes the need for the project and identifies funding, the CIP committee approves the project and your office chief assigns you the project. You will then contact the director and head maintenance technician to go over any project details. At this point they become the primary users for the project.

- Deputy maintenance director: As second in command, this person will work with PMs to confirm project specifications based on their ability to do some of the work in house. They may be able to perform project tasks related to carpet removal and/or installation, fueling of generators, striping a parking lot, vinyl composite tile (VCT), painting of interior and exterior spaces, and any work that may be performed by maintenance during construction. Once this work is identified as work performed by the owner, this work will need to be coordinated within or outside of the main project. For instance, the project manager may ask maintenance to remove a raised computer floor, or demo a door before the contractor shows up to perform contracted work. To save money, maintenance may be able to provide and install finishes.
- HVAC master technician: When a project manager identifies a need for mechanical, heating, and cooling equipment related to their project, the PM will engage the person who will be the end user maintaining the equipment. This technician will also be the PM's contact when reviewing specifications and drawings related to HVAC systems and equipment.
- Master electrician technician and master plumber: As with the HVAC master technician, an electrical technician, usually a certified master electrician, will work with the PM by reviewing the electrical equipment specifications and drawings so that they meet county standard operating procedures (SOP). The master plumber technician will provide the same expertise when developing equipment specifications and drawings.
- Locksmith: Any keying requirements will need to be coordinated with the keying technician. They will specify the equipment and keying types per the organization's SOP. The PM will coordinate meetings with the keying technician, design firm, and users so that keying hardware is identified and specified correctly.

14. Department of construction management and inspection (DCMI)/construction management (CM): DCMI oversees and inspects every aspect of all construction-related activities associated with a CIP project. Working with a PM, DCMI helps identify and resolve any issues that arise during construction to ensure that the project is completed per the plans and specifications. Some organizations do not have such a department and instead will hire a construction management firm to provide the

same services. Project managers work in coordination with the on-site construction inspector by attending progress meetings and coordinating RFI responses from the design team back to the contractor. Construction management inspectors do the following:

- Perform reviews for scope verification, scope baseline, activity sequencing, activity duration estimating, activity durations, assign activity identifiers, and constructability.
- Along with the PM, the inspector helps monitor and control project work, only during construction.
- Inspect work and materials per specifications and approved submittals.
- Keep track of and monitor construction progress and any risk triggers through verification techniques and variance analysis.
- Provide quality assurance (QA) inspections and performance reporting for work performed by contractors/sellers.
- Track percent completion (PC or PCT) for time and construction.
- Document the start date (SD), start-to-finish (SF), start-to-start (SS), planned finish date (PF), planned start date (PS), remaining durations (RDs), schedule finish date (SF), schedule start date (SS), all target completion dates (TC), target finish date (TF), target start date (TS), and revise the project calendar during construction.
- Track all construction schedule activities including data dates (DD), that is, time-now date, finish dates, finish-to-finish, and finish-to-start (FS); review and develop logic diagrams and logical relationships in the construction schedule; review network diagrams of construction activities such as the schedule of values (SOV); and identify any lead/lag time, total float, slack, or near-critical activities in the construction schedule. They also perform a network analysis regarding the construction network path and identify any subnetworks.
- Perform technical performance measurement techniques that include construction progress reports.
- Perform root cause analysis.
- Identify potential threshold limits during construction.
- Provide schedule control.
- Perform rolling wave planning with the PM.
- Generate daily field reports.
- Track RFIs from the contractor to the design team and if the response requires additional work, manage the construction change order process, also known as scope control, and identify any scope creep or scope changes.
- Determine the need, negotiate the price, and process proposed change orders (PCOs).

- Manage the submittal log.
- Approve pay requisitions based on the contractor's progress and a previously approved schedule of values and track the latest revised estimate or estimate at completion (EAC).
- Generate substantial completion documents.
- Determine reductions in bonding and retainage as work is completed according to the schedule of values.
- Develop as-builts with the contractor and architect at the end of work.

  It is important to note that the inspector and the project manager work together throughout the construction phase of a project since the project manager is the gatekeeper of the control account (CA) during design, and then the inspector becomes the gatekeeper of the control account during construction, with the PM providing direction and support.

15. Risk management department: Risk management is a hardly noticed department until something catastrophic happens. They work with project managers to establish and make sure safety standards are incorporated into the project, and in conjunction with DCMI, make sure contractors follow OSHA standards and regulations during construction, and apply for any required supplemental insurance prior to and during construction.

16. Permits office: Of all the departments listed here, permits offices have the most potential to hold up your project during design and construction. With as much, and in some cases, more power than the BOCC, they can kill your project with excessive regulation, additional submissions, and fees. It is of the upmost importance that your design firms know the process and follow the rules regarding submissions, fees, and responses and/or revisions to comments.

17. Interagency information technologies (IIT) department: Many organizations have IIT departments that are responsible for telecommunications, intrusion systems, and card reader access doors for building security, along with computer set-ups. They may require a special room or closet to house these components, and they must be incorporated into the final design documents. As with maintenance, IIT departments have standard equipment and requirements. For example, our IIT department requires us to provide a 4 x 8 sheet of fireproof plywood in an IIT closet for mounting components and install a spot-cooling unit to keep equipment in their specified operational temperature range.

18. Architect/engineer (A/E): Along with an architect, who acts as a general contractor for the design team and is the gatekeeper for design development and coordination, there will be a team of engineers that may consist of civil, structural, mechanical, plumbing, electrical, geotechnical, surveyor, interior design, cost estimator, and environmental engineers. All

of the subconsultants work under the direction of the architect who in turn works for the organization's authorized representatives.

19. Interviewers/evaluators (throughout this book, the term *interviewers/ evaluators* means "evaluators"): Using a quasi-Delphi technique as defined in the *PMBOK* Guide,[10] this group who, unlike a Delphi group, knows who the evaluators are, typically consists of four staff members engaged in the task of reviewing, evaluating, and ranking firms that apply for SOQs and RFPs. The purchasing manager is the organizer for these activities only as a facilitator. The four evaluators consist of a user's representative, other project managers, or people familiar with these tasks.

LINES OF COMMUNICATION

Because many lines of communication exist on any project, keeping track can become confusing. The *Project Management Professional Study Guide* provides a formula for calculating the required number of communication lines as follows:[11]

(number of participants (number of participants less one)) divided by two.
$$(n \times (n - 1)) \div 2$$
So for example, if we have 10 participants, we would have the following:
$$(10 \times (10 - 1)) \div 2 = 45 \text{ lines of communication}$$

Throughout a project your communication priorities will change as you start and finish milestones, phases, and tasks, so with each phase you may need to redefine your lines of communication to limit confusion. Since we are starting at the very beginning of a project, you need to identify the users that will help you through the process of obtaining design phase services. Let's say you are soliciting the services of a design firm for the fire station shown in figure 1.1. In using the list of key players above, and knowing that Jack Smith is the fire company's contact for this project, you develop a list of users who will be directly involved in making decisions that will move your project through the design phase process. Based on how your organization is structured departmentally, they may include the following representatives during design, construction, or both phases:

1. Jack Smith, anytown fire company #1 representative (design and construction)
2. Purchasing department (design and construction)
3. Maintenance department (design and construction)

4. IIT (design and construction)
5. Management services department (design and construction)
6. Construction management inspector (bidding phase and construction)
7. Facilities management department (95% construction documents (CDs) and construction)
8. Office chief/engineering manager (cc only as a secondary recipient) (design and construction)
9. General contractor (GC) (construction)
10. Design firm architect/engineer (A/E) (design and construction)

PROCUREMENT CONTRACTS FOR DESIGN AND CONSTRUCTION

Contracts are commonly used during design and construction to provide an agreement that will pay the supplier, or seller, of goods or services based on their performance in accordance with the project specifications, that is, the directions.

Contracts can be identified as three common types that include various derivatives of these types.

The *PMBOK Guide*[12] defines contracts of different types that can be used to execute a project as follows:

1. Fixed-price/lump-sum contracts: Predominately used in CIP design and construction contracts, a lump-sum price is paid throughout a project based on milestones. To use this type of contract, the project must have a very detailed scope of work.
   - Firm-fixed-price (FFP) contract: This is a popular type of contract used for competitively bidding on a project for design and/or construction. This is a preferred contract type because it fosters competition between bidders and encourages fair pricing. Progress payments, after the contract is executed, will be identified and outlined in the front-end portion of the specifications (see appendix D).
   - Fixed-price-incentive-fee (FPIF) contract: Similar to the FFP contract, it includes some type of bonus. Monetary incentives can be provided in this type of contract for early completion of a project or if the product is provided under budget. Keep in mind that the owner assumes more risk here, because early delivery may not be possible while on-time delivery is.
   - Fixed-price/economic price adjustment contract: This contract allows the same benefits as a lump-sum contract with a stipulation allowing adjustments to certain materials that fluctuate in price due to economic

conditions. For example, you may allow the contract to include a price adjustment agreement for hot-mixed asphalt stating that a cost adjustment either up or down will govern the quantity price based on the current cost price index for that material. Copper can also be an item requiring a cost adjustment.

- Fixed-price redetermination contract: Used more for R&D projects, this type of contract allows the negotiation of a fair price for an immediate need but not for subsequent phases of a project. The prices for other phases need to be determined via contract negotiations after the first phase is completed. When negotiating, if a fair price cannot be established, a fee not to exceed price is established and the actual cost is paid based on the actual work performed after completion of the specified milestones throughout the project.

2. Cost reimbursement contracts
    - Cost-plus-fee (CPF)/cost-plus-percentage of cost (CPPC) contracts: These contracts allow for invoicing based on the actual cost of the labor and material, with the profit invoiced once the project is completed. This provides an incentive to complete the project as soon as possible. The seller is reimbursed for allowable costs plus a fee that's calculated as a percentage of costs. Obviously, there is no incentive for the seller to complete the work quickly with this type of contract.
    - Cost-plus-fixed fee (CPFF) contract: Used predominantly in CIP projects, this contract allows for payment to a vendor based on a lump-sum cost that does not change unless a change in the original SOW is required or requested.
    - Cost-plus-incentive fee (CPIF) contract: Similar to the cost-plus contract, it allows the vendor to invoice for work based on a predetermined amount of time and material. The vendor will be paid based on a user/vendor ratio. If the target cost is exceeded, the vendor's profit decreases. If the target costs are less than originally estimated, the vendor's profit increases.

3. Time and material (T&M) contract: If you combine a fixed-price contract with a cost-reimbursable contract, you would have a T&M contract. It allows you to execute a contract even though you do not know exactly what the final cost will be. For example, you may have a need for a service at a cost per hour rate over a certain amount of time. After the time has been exhausted, there may be additional hours required for services that were unknown during the time the contract was made. Thus a cost reimbursement would be required for any additional work over and above what was originally estimated. Some organizations use a "fee not to exceed" stipulation in conjunction with this type of contract. Then if the vendor

starts getting close to exceeding the fee, they would simply have the firm provide a fee proposal to finish the work and process a change order.

Keep in mind that with CIP construction projects, a fixed-fee/lump-sum contract is predominantly used. However, in some cases, a T&M contract is used under an indefinite quantity (IDQ) contract with a fee not to exceed clause built into the contract, allowing the PM to obtain a fee proposal breakdown represented in hours to perform each task of the scope of work; this will be used to generate a purchase order for the work to be billed against. Contracts can be very detailed or only one page (see appendix B for a sample design contract). We use them both, depending on the size and scope of a project. Your supervisor, purchasing manager, and legal department need to approve any contracts not previously used. Use of a short or long contract, developed by your organization, can be beneficial when executing small projects. It is important to mention that some boilerplate contracts, such as Engineers Joint Contract Documents Committee (EJCDC) contract documents (see appendix E for a sample construction contract) are generalized for architectural/engineering or construction contracts, and can be viewed at their respective websites. In order to make contracts fit an organization's rules and standards, a supplemental contract to the original contract may need to be developed and approved by your legal department to allow the organization flexibility to modify it for a specific need (see appendix D). This finalized and approved document will form the foundation of how and what work will be provided, clearly identifying the roles and responsibilities of the owner and the design firm and/or contractor. A draft of the contract should be included when soliciting bids under an RFP, IDQ, or RFQs.

OTHER TYPES OF CONTRACTS

- Letters contract: Used if an immediate need for services or goods is required and a typical contract cannot be established due to time constraints.
- Basic ordering agreements (BOAs)/indefinite delivery contract: Allows awarding one or more suppliers for the same services or goods.
  - Definite quantity contract (DQC): Allows the supplier to price goods or services over a period of time, thus locking in the fees for items to be delivered to assigned locations. Also, the supplies or services need to be regularly available or will be available after a short lead time.
  - Requirements contract: Provides for filling all purchase requirements of a designated organization's activities for supplies or services during a specified time, with deliveries to be scheduled by placing orders only

with one designated contractor. For instance, a general contractor may enter into this type of contract with a supplier of nails and for a designated period of time, the supplier will provide specified goods delivered at a specified location based on a previously agreed-upon price.

- Indefinite quantity contract (IDQ): Provides for an indefinite quantity, with stated limits, of specific supplies or services to be furnished during a fixed period, with deliveries to be scheduled by placing orders with the contractor. The contract shall require the organization to order and the contractor to furnish at least a stated minimum quantity of supplies or services, and, if ordered, the contractor to furnish any additional quantities, not to exceed a stated maximum sum.
- Task order contract: A contract for a service that does not procure or specify an established quantity of services (other than a minimum or maximum quantity) and that provides for issuance of orders for the performance of tasks during the period of the contract.
- Delivery/task order contract: A contract for supplies that does not procure or specify an exact quantity (other than a minimum or maximum quantity) and that provides for the issuance of orders for the delivery of supplies during the period of the contract. Task and delivery order contracting should be used when the project officer anticipates recurring requirements but cannot determine in advance the precise quantities of services or supplies that will be required during the contract period of performance. In general, task and delivery order contracting may be used to acquire any type of service or supply item. However, this method should not be used in instances where a fixed-price contract or a cost-type contract ordinarily would be used (i.e., a specified level of service has been established prior to awarding a contract).

DESIGN/BUILD CONTRACTS

Used in the construction industry, design/build contracts allow for the designer and builder to perform project requirements as one entity responsible for all required project tasks, from design to use and occupancy by the users, as opposed to the standard method of design-bid-build. Using a design/build contract will eliminate change orders regarding design errors and/or omissions. However, user-requested and unforeseen change orders may be required.

Design/builders have amassed impressive results from past projects showing that they can complete work faster and provide better quality at a lower cost, along with providing better communication efficiencies. However, some drawbacks when using a design/build contract can be the lack of competition between bidders because they will not be using the same designs. Also, building contractors typically do not have registered designers on staff and will need to subcontract with a design firm, creating some issues regarding insurance coverage.

If engaging in this type of contract, be sure the design firm has errors and omissions insurance that do not exclude construction services. If their insurance company cannot provide this coverage, then incorporating language in the contract will be required. Conversely, the contract will need to contain language stating the contractor will need to be covered regarding professional design services.

FEASIBILITY STUDY

A feasibility study/space study can include many types of work that will allow your organization to make a better-educated decision and minimize potential risks. The study could include, but is not limited to, the following:

- Space study: How much square feet is needed for operation?
- Environmental site design (ESD): This study determines what impacts the project may have on the environment, and what can be done to mitigate any potential environmental issues to the maximum extent possible.
- Phase I archeological study: This will determine if evidence exists that makes the area a historic site, which could cause a delay. A phase II or III may be required based on the phase I findings, which can cause a project to be on hold for months or even years.
- Traffic studies: Proposed intersections onto existing roadways may need acceleration/deceleration lanes and to perform site distance and speed studies.
- Geotechnical services: Borings may be required to determine the location of underground structures and utilities, along with soils reports. A recommended foundation and pavement design may also be required.

If land has been identified for a project and the land acquisition coordinator feels that the land can be obtained, the organization may need a feasibility study to see if the proposed structure fits the site. Before the organization buys the land, a program needs to be developed to identify building space and total building square footage needed. In order to provide the feasibility study, you may need to develop a scope of work and request fees using an IDQ. An IDQ contract is an agreement that allows a project manager to order services within the established limits of the IDQ. Task orders are then used to execute the work per the IDQ contracted services.

Using our sample project in figure 1.1, we can request a feasibility study to develop a program for the new fire station based on land designated for that purpose. The study will provide information determining if the site is able to support all the components for construction of the fire station on a proposed site. It is important to remember that if you are using an IDQ architect to develop documents that will later be used in an RFP to further design the station, the IDQ architect is not permitted to bid on the RFP due to purchasing rules, conflicts of interest, and fairness.

Most organizations have procedures developed regarding space allocations when developing a new or renovated building project. For example, my organization has a standard operating procedure (SOP), rules to follow when allocating elements that are of primary consideration for requesting space, providing a guide when identifying spaces and performing floor plan layouts.

When analyzing potential space requirements, your organization will need to know some key elements related to the basis for the requested space. They are as follows:

- General justification for the requirement: Have you simply run out of space due to your organization's growth, or need to repair, maintain, upgrade, or expand an existing space?
- Type of space: Is it an office, storage facility, parking garage, school, or other facility?
- Quality of space: Will the finishes be opulent or economical? Is this a rental space? If so, what is the rate? Geographical location can also dictate quality and cost of space. For example, space located in downtown Manhattan is more expensive than in downtown Pittsburgh.
- Amount of space: What is the overall square footage required to accommodate expansion including staff, equipment, storage, parking, and circulation throughout the building? (Circulation is usually calculated by adding a percentage of additional square footage to a space so that people can move through the space without blocking egress paths. For office space we typically add 10% to 15% for circulation around furnishings and equipment in the space).
- Location of space: Is this a new building or an existing building being renovated? If it is a new building, does your organization own the land, and will the land meet the criteria required by planning and zoning regulations?

If you are requesting a space study be performed by a design firm, you will need to provide them with the answers to the questions above, along with a list of the allowable space allocations and furniture approved by your organization.

DESIGN DOCUMENTS

As defined in the *PMBOK Guide*,[13] progressive elaboration is a similar technique used to review design phases. Design phase services establish documents required for review and approval by the users, allowing a minimum of two weeks for review of each submission and three weeks for the 95% review before moving on to the next submission. Standard guidelines for submittals are as follows:

- Schematic design: Based on the findings of the feasibility study, the design firm provides an initial design that meets all the preliminary requirements of zoning a site plan and acquiring approval by a planning commission, or other approval agencies. This is sometimes done in combination with the 35% design development documents.
- 35% design development (35% DDs): After schematic design review and approval by the project management team, the designer proceeds to develop documents that establish the footprint of the building and development of all required utility plans. Depending on project scope, a cost estimate may be required. The site planning permit process should start at this stage of design process.
- 50% construction documents (50% CDs): You will start to see interior walls and elevations during this stage of design review and approval. At this point you can still move non-loadbearing walls and enhance or eliminate elements of the design. Some of the building standards checklist items should start to be evident in the documents. A construction estimate should be provided at this stage of design.
- 95% construction documents (95% CDs): Coordination drawings, details, and final specifications are reviewed at this stage. An additional cost estimate may be required.
- 100% bid documents: The architect will provide the final set of stamped drawings and specifications for advertisement of your project. You will need to distribute copies to your office chief, purchasing, maintenance, management services, construction management, and the user agency.
- Bid phase services: Purchasing will be the lead agency when advertising the project. They will work with the project manager in responding to questions the contractors may have during the bidding process. When addenda need to be published, the same format as the construction documents and project manual should be followed by referencing the answer per the numbering system in the project manual.
- Construction administration services (CA): Once an award is executed, the architect will approve any submittals, provide responses to RFIs from the

contractor, and provide any assistance that may be required during the construction phase of the project.

- As-built drawings: Construction management, along with the contractor, will be tasked with providing a set of redlined drawings indicating any deviations from the original drawings. This will help maintenance in the future if they need more exact information regarding locations of mechanical, electrical, and plumbing (MEP) equipment. They will turn those drawings over to the design firm so they can develop a final set of as-built drawings.

COST ESTIMATES

The purpose of a cost estimate is to make sure the design is progressing within the established construction budget that was previously approved by the organization and outlined in the RFP to the designer during the bid process. As part of their contract, the design firm is required to provide either a professional third-party estimate or an in-house cost estimate. Either way, the cost, based on the documents submitted, must be within the established budget or re-evaluation and redesign will be required at no additional cost to the organization.

The *PMBOK Guide* defines cost estimates of different types that can be used to identify project costs as follows:[14]

- Rough order of magnitude estimate (ROM): In CIP construction, project managers do not use this type of estimate due to its range of -50 to +100%, but this would be a good estimating method to use during brainstorming so that later it would be developed to become more accurate in a range of -10 to +15%.
- Analogous estimating: CIP construction refers to this as a 15% schematic and 35% design development cost estimate, and it is a method of estimating work packages based on historical data of similar projects and relies on expert judgment, if done in-house. A third-party professional estimator would use a better developed ROM, that is, -10 to +15% accuracy.
- Bottom-up estimating: CIP construction refers to this as a 50% construction documents cost estimate and is a method of estimating a component of work. The work is decomposed into more detail. An estimate is prepared of what is needed to meet the requirements of each of the lower, more detailed pieces of work, and these estimates are then aggregated into a total quantity for the component of work. The accuracy of bottom-up estimating is driven

by the size and complexity of the work identified at the lower levels. Generally, smaller work scopes increase the accuracy of the estimates.

- Parametric estimating: The CIP construction term is a 95% construction documents cost estimate, and it is a estimating technique that uses a statistical relationship between historical data and other variables (e.g., square footage in construction, lines of code in software development) to calculate an estimate for activity parameters, such as scope, cost, budget, and duration. This technique can produce higher levels of accuracy depending upon the sophistication and the underlying data built into the model. An example for the cost parameter is multiplying the planned quantity of work to be performed by the historical cost per unit to obtain the estimated cost.

In my office, at a minimum, and if we have more than three phases of design, we direct the design firm to provide estimates performed by a professional third-party firm that specializes in estimating, using an analogous estimating method for 35% design documents, a bottom-up method of estimation for the 50% CD design construction cost estimate, and a parametric estimate for 95% CD submission. In some cases, a definitive estimate may be needed before bidding the project.

PERMITS

Since the permit offices I encounter are very large divisions, I will use them as an example when describing the different layers of the permit process.

When a design reaches a certain level of detail, the design firm will apply for permits with the organization paying the fees. In some cases, the design firm will pay the fees and charge it back to the projects reimbursable expenses. Reimbursable expenses will be covered in more detail in chapter 4.

Permit departments are set up to review, approve, and inspect projects from site plan approval through construction and final use and occupancy (U&O). The permit process during design is long, about nine weeks for site plan approval and eight weeks for building permit approval before permits for construction are issued. The PM will interact with many offices in the permit departments to make sure the design firm is applying for permits in the proper order. It is important that permits track concurrently with your design submissions so that once the bid set is finalized, permits should be approved. Do not ever go to construction bid without having building permits in hand first. Below is an outline of how a permit department processes a project through their approval system:

- Preliminary site plan (submission and approval through planning and zoning): When applying for site plan approval, the design firm or PM will apply for a site plan review. Once fees are paid, the planning office will assign a planner to decide if your preliminary site plan requires a staff level review or planning commission approval. This process can take as long as two to three months.
- Adequate public facilities ordinance (APFO): APFO is becoming more popular throughout the country to promote smart growth. Some governments do not require APFO as part of site plan approval. During site plan review, and as a requirement for site plan approval, the design firm or PM will need to apply for an APFO permit. An administrator will review your proposed site plan to see if your project will require improvements that need to be in place before construction can start. This can include infrastructure such as roads, water and sewer line extensions, or even land set aside for future use by the governing organization. Some developers have even been required to provide a certain amount of funds for future support buildings, such as a school.
- Forest resource ordinance (FRO): During site plan review, FRO is applied for and reviewed. This ordinance may not be required in your state. In Maryland, FRO was developed to preserve forested land. If a developer, in this case, your organization, and you acting as a developer, develops on any land in that jurisdiction, they are required to set aside a percentage of forested land and place it in an easement to protect it from future development. Rules also exist if no forest is on the land being developed. The developer can choose to use forest banking credits and provide payment to the jurisdiction's banking trust fund, called a "fee-in-lieu" payment.
- Environmental site design submission (concept plan): A concept plan is the initial site design submission to the permits office regarding how the engineer intends to address any stormwater management issues to the maximum extent possible.
- Site plan approval, round one, including APFO and FRO: Planning commissions are made up of citizens whose vote is based on a project meeting the standards outlined in their adopted zoning regulations. APFO and FRO are approved based on the recommendations of planning department staff. Before and during a planning commission meeting, planning commissioners will vote to approve your plans, or require more design and a second round of submissions before approval. Since they only meet once a month, you may end up revising your design schedule due to losing a month before you can move to the next stage in the permit process. This is why it is important to hire a firm that is familiar with your jurisdiction's permitting process and regulations.

- Improvement plans: Once site plan approval is granted, your design firm needs to start the process of submitting improvement plans for review. Fees are paid by the design firm or the organization. These are construction drawings related to how much stormwater management may be required for your project. If a stormwater management design is required, you will have rules that need to be followed as outlined by the permit department.
- Soil conservation services (SCS): In Maryland, we are required to submit plans to the state's soil conservation district (SCD) to make sure no erosion of soil will take place during and after construction. This is called a sediment and erosion control plan.
- Environmental compliance section (ECS): Once SCD approves the drawings, an application is made for a major or minor grading permit based on your sediment and erosion control plan. ECS will review and approve the plans, then set up a site meeting with the contractor to go over the plans and inspect the sediment and erosion control devices along with verifying the limits of disturbance (LOD), silt fence inspections to make sure the soil control plan is in agreement with the plans, and stable construction entrances, after they are in place and before starting construction. Once ECS agrees that the site is now in compliance with the plan, the contractor can start construction, assuming that the building permits have all been approved. After the construction project is completed, ECS will require a set of as-built drawings showing the completed stormwater management (SWM) facilities.
- Notice of intent (NOI) permit: This is used in Maryland to inform the state's Department of Environment (MDE) that a construction project will be disturbing land in excess of 1 acre. Your state may not require this. Additionally, national pollution discharge elimination system (NPDES) rules, as part of the clean water act (CWA), 1972 amendments, requires the same rule of notification procedures for disturbances over 1 acre.
- Non-tidal wetlands permit: As with an NOI permit, this is a state permit that may not be required in your state. Check with local jurisdictions that enforce codes and ordinances. It is a way of protecting wetlands and any native species of plants and animals that might be facing extinction.
- Building permits office: Building reviews are started once the design has reached a certain level of detail. At 95% CDs, the design firm will apply for building permits. The permit reviewer will stamp the plans as approved once they comply with all required codes.
- Building inspector: Once approved plans are accepted, building inspectors will perform inspections throughout construction. Along with the building inspector, you may also need inspections from a fire marshal, life safety officer, electrical and plumbing inspectors, and health department inspectors. You will need all their approvals at certain stages of construction in order to obtain use and occupancy (U&O) approval.

2

Statement of Qualifications (SOQ) Long List

You will find that some of the tasks and phases in this book will require more of your attention than others. This chapter requires a substantial chunk of time on your part. Bidding for services is one of the most important tasks performed by a project manager; it can set a positive or negative tone throughout the whole project. Being optimistic will help you gain the support needed to motivate the other project team members. You can burn up tons of time and resources during this phase of a project. The saying "You're only as strong as your weakest link" definitely applies here. The PM may encounter many threats and will be at the mercy of and reliant on other staff or team members who all have different priorities, making it difficult to keep the process of developing a short list moving efficiently through the product life cycle. It is during this process that you will determine what requests to use. With direction from your organization's purchasing manager, you can develop/advertise for services by way of the following requests for services:

- Indefinite quantity contract (IDQ) (see appendix C): Used when undetermined amounts of time are required to perform tasks. We use IDQs to perform space studies, preliminary site plan review, geotechnical services, traffic studies, and more.
- Statement of qualifications (SOQ): Used to execute an initial request for services to develop a short list. It provides the PM and the evaluators the most up-to-date information on firms interested in bidding for services.
- Request for proposal (RFP): Used in a similar capacity as an SOQ, a RFP is developed and used for assessment of the short-listed firms that made it through the SOQ process. The RFP will include two sections of scoring. The first is the technical and interview section. The second is the fee proposal.

• Request for quote (RFQ): PMs occasionally are assigned partial projects that do not require an SOQ or RFP to obtain services. RFQs are used in these cases to request a quote based on approved purchasing rules, usually to obtain three or five bids depending on the quantity and cost of work requested, or by using an approved IDQ contract that does not require a three to five bid process, but rather a fee proposal from the design firm by way of a task order request. Services requested could include space studies, geotechnical work, site plan design options, title searches, and traffic studies. Remember that keeping excellent written records of phone conversations, e-mails, and meeting minutes are necessary so that you, or your organization, can refer to those documents at a later date.

INTERVIEWER/EVALUATOR APPROVAL BY A CONSULTANT SELECTION COMMITTEE (CSC)

In some organizations there is a consultant selection committee (CSC) made up of fellow employees experienced in the consultant selection process. They work in conjunction with the finance department, purchasing, and the CSC committee.

Most CSCs will communicate with your supervisors. The committee meets once a month, and maybe less often, depending on the amount of CIP projects needing execution in a given fiscal year. Given that the committee has performed most of the groundwork in assigning project priorities, your involvement with the committee may be limited. The only direct interaction you might have with the CSC committee is in regard to requests for approval of a recommended list of potential evaluators, with purchasing manager concurrence. In my organization, the purchasing manager directs the PM to provide a written request, typically by e-mail, to the CSC for approval of the list of evaluators.

Assigning evaluators based on the information in figure 1.1, and following the rules of the CSC committee and purchasing department, the PM will forward a written request to the purchasing manager informing them that the CIP project, Anytown Fire Company #1 fire station, is ready to begin the bidding process for obtaining design services. With purchasing approval, the PM develops a request for evaluators. The evaluators will likely consist of a user representative, other PMs familiar with the selection process, and you.

STATEMENT OF QUALIFICATIONS (SOQ)

SOQs (see appendix A) are requested by a PM through the purchasing department when a project requires design services. Developing an SOQ requires knowledge of your organization's purchasing department hierarchy and rules, along with background knowledge of the services requested. This is where you will need to coordinate with a purchasing department representative. The purchasing manager will be your counterpart and gatekeeper in monitoring the SOQ process, based on their procurement documents, procurement management plan, and procurement rules. The purchasing department establishes dates to advertise the SOQ, collects and distributes the information provided by the perspective firm to the evaluators, and then organizes and ranks the firms, based on evaluator scores, to develop a short list of candidates. Usually the top four or five firms qualify for the next round, the short list, of the selection process.

An SOQ document should include information that firms can respond to with accurate and current information. Using our sample project shown in figure 1.1, you would produce an SOQ document similar to that shown in appendix A and include the following:

- Cover page: The organization's information, date, bid number, and what the SOQ is for
- Due date: This will let the firms know when proposals are due
- Purpose: Describes why the organization is requesting letters of interest for services and identifying what is being built
- Background: Provides a brief history of how the organization determined a need for the services requested and gives general details of what is to be built
- Selection process: Provides firms interested with details about how the selection process will be conducted
- Scope of services: Lists and describes the tasks that the firm will be providing, along with necessary design disciplines
- Design and construction budget: Provides the approved design and construction budget amounts
- Evaluation criteria: Establishes criteria that most benefits the project and assigns weighted scores that reflect their importance
- Submittal requirements: Specific set of directions to follow when firms submit their information

Criteria used for evaluations are most likely already developed and in place as a boilerplate document at your PMO that can be revised with minor changes to fit your project. Figure 2.1 shows a sample cover sheet.

SOQ ADVERTISEMENT

Working with your purchasing department, the PM will finalize the SOQ document and the purchasing manager will post the project for advertisement. The length of time used to produce and advertise the SOQ can take as little as

---

(Organizations logo)

(ORGANIZATION IDENTIFICATION)

February 03, 2006

SOQ No. xx-xxx-xx

REQUEST FOR STATEMENTS OF QUALIFICATION
And
LETTERS OF INTEREST
For
ARCHITECTURAL/ENGINEERING SERVICES
For
INDEPENDENT FIRE COMPANY #1 FIRE STATION

Statements of Qualification are due: **March 1, 2006** by 4pm local time

---

Figure 2.1

two weeks or as long as a month. Part of the purchasing department's job is to collect any requests for information (RFIs) from design firms and route them to the PM for review and response. Responses need to be provided in an order that corresponds with the numbering format of the SOQ. From advertisement to contract signing, the purchasing manager will be the gatekeeper for all these activities. SOQ responses from the design firms should be prepared simply and economically, providing a straightforward, concise description of the firm's skills, experience, and capabilities to satisfy the organization's need for design services. Emphasis should be on completeness and clarity of content. Only firms that provide evidence of having successfully performed the desired services should receive further consideration. For example, if your organization desires a firm specialized in fire stations, you may not want one that has only provided residential design services.

In the solicitation requirements, clear direction on how to submit their proposal should include one unbound original copy and one electronic copy in your desired format. Also, an electronic copy should be submitted in a single file on a CD or USB flash drive. This will make gathering and routing the documents to the evaluators more expeditious. The unbound original that they submit on standard 8½" × 11" paper should be labeled on the outside with the SOQ title, bid number, and the name of the firm.

Firms need to format their SOQ responses in a manner that is identical to the information provided so that it corresponds directly to, and is identified with, the numbering scheme of the SOQ. This will make reviews quicker and more concise in the individual evaluation of each firm. This is especially helpful when you have 30 firms to review.

SOQ SCORING CRITERIA

During the process of selecting a design firm, and using our sample project, fire station design services consist of two steps, the first of which is this SOQ process and the second, the RFP process. With responses received and distributed to the evaluators, the PM and evaluation team will identify a short list of the firms they believe to be best qualified in providing the needed services based on their relative merits. The team will conduct a final selection process after the short-listing process has been completed.

Only those firms short-listed will be invited to participate in the second step of the selection process. The methodology of the final selection process consists of issuing a RFP, which includes interviews, fee evaluations, and/or other means determined to be in the best interests of the organization.

When all interested design firms provide their qualifications, purchasing will distribute their information to the evaluators approved by the CSC. Working with your purchasing manager, the PM will have developed a SOQ that informs the potential design firms how their information is scored, referring to the sample scoring sheet in the sample SOQ. This is the initial evaluation form and scoring criteria based on services outlined therein. Individual evaluator's comments need to be recorded on an evaluation forms similar to those shown in figures 2.2.1–2.2.5.

Using our sample SOQ in appendix A and figure 2.1, we can direct the evaluators to score firms based on the following technical information:

1. Firm experience: This is based on the firm's professional qualifications needed to successfully and satisfactorily perform the required services and provide evidence that the most recent project experience and past performance on projects containing similar scopes of work were successfully completed.
2. Firm or practice professional qualifications: The firms need to identify the team of professionals to be used in providing the necessary services.

SOQ (insert number) Statements of Qualification/ Letters of Interest for A/E Services for Fire Station Design	Name of Firm:_____ Evaluator:_____

INITIAL EVALUATION FORM

Total Points Awarded: ____ of 100

Criterion A: Firm experience, professional qualification necessary for satisfactory performance of required services, and past performance on similar projects. (total of 70 points)

A.1.1, A.1.2, A.1.3, A.1.4

Note: Items A.1.1 through A.1.4 do not carry any points. Identify any issues of concern you have, if any, regarding the firm's response to these categories in the space below.

_____
_____
_____
_____
_____
_____
_____
_____

A.1.5 Firm experience in providing similar A/E services

Notes: Score: ____ of 10 points

_____
_____
_____
_____
_____
_____
_____
_____

Figure 2.2.1

SOQ 10-CSC-01 Statements of Qualification/ Letters of Interest for A/E Services for Fire Station Design	Name of Firm:_____ Evaluator:_____

INITIAL EVALUATION FORM

A.2 Professional Qualifications necessary for satisfactory performance of required services (for A.2.1 through A.2.12)

Notes: Score: _____ of 25 points

_____
_____
_____
_____
_____
_____
_____
_____
_____
_____
_____
_____
_____
_____

A.3.1 Five most recently completed projects

Notes: Score: _____ of 10 points

_____
_____
_____
_____
_____
_____
_____
_____
_____
_____
_____
_____

Figure 2.2.2

SOQ 10-CSC-01 Statements of Qualification/ Letters of Interest for A/E Services for Fire Station Design	Name of Firm:_____ Evaluator:_____

INITIAL EVALUATION FORM

A.3.2 Five most similar projects

Notes: Score: _____ of 25 points

_____
_____
_____
_____
_____
_____
_____
_____
_____
_____
_____
_____
_____
_____

Criteria B: Demonstrated capacity to accomplish the work in the required time

B.1 and B.2

Note: Items B.1 through B.2 do not carry any points. Identify any issues of concern you have, if any, regarding the firm's response to these categories in the space below.

_____
_____
_____
_____
_____
_____
_____
_____

Figure 2.2.3

SOQ 10-CSC-01	Name of
Statements of Qualification/	Firm:_____
Letters of Interest for	
A/E Services for Fire Station Design	Evaluator:_____

INITIAL EVALUATION FORM

B.3 Ability to accomplish work as contracted – past projects in A.3.1

Notes: Score: _____ of 10 points

_____
_____
_____
_____
_____
_____
_____
_____

B.4 Ability to accomplish work as contracted – most similar projects in A.3.2

Notes: Score: _____ of 10 points

_____
_____
_____
_____
_____
_____
_____

Figure 2.2.4

SOQ 10-CSC-01	Name of
Statements of Qualification/	Firm:_____
Letters of Interest for	
A/E Services for Fire Station Design	Evaluator:_____

INITIAL EVALUATION FORM

Criteria C: Local Knowledge

C.1 Familiarity with local geographic area
C.2 Familiarity with Frederick County's construction, design, review and permitting procedures

Notes: Score: ____ of 10 points

_____
_____
_____
_____
_____
_____
_____
_____
_____
_____

Figure 2.2.5

Subconsultants need to provide the qualifications of their personnel to be used on a project and forward these to the firm applying for the SOQ, so that they can publish the information in the format as directed. Qualifications of subconsultants should contain the personnel proposed to work on the project, including position description, education, active registrations in the state that the work is being performed, experience, and qualification relevant to the scope of work. The federal government standard forms 254 and 255 or standard form 330 is often requested.

3. Five most recently completed projects: These projects need to match, as closely as possible, the type of project being designed. For instance, if an organization is requesting design services for a new fire station and they list five school projects, they should not score well on this criterion because the uses are very different operationally for these building types.

4. Five most similar projects: The same applies here as stated in the five most recently completed projects. For example, some firms may have worked on many fire stations in the past, but not recently, and those projects should be listed here.

5. Capacity to accomplish the work in the required time: Many firms that apply for your projects may be overworked, undersized, or both. By requesting current workloads of staff and their subconsultants, you can better determine if they have the resources available to accomplish your project goals.
6. Ability to accomplish work on past projects: This will give you an indication of how well the firm is staffed and how efficient it is. Keep in mind that sometimes smaller is better. In a smaller firm the principal may also act as their project manager, thus eliminating a layer of bureaucracy, but also be aware that workload can be an issue in small firms that might take on too much work at the same time.
7. Ability to accomplish work on most similar projects: As stated in the ability to accomplish work on past projects, evaluators can make better determinations about the firm.
8. Local knowledge: Familiarity with your project's location is critical. If you have a firm that is not local, meaning not located in the same county as your project, they may be seen as not being as familiar with local general contractors, local material suppliers, permits people, and subcontractors. This should not be a negative if they have worked with these entities mentioned.
9. Experience with the local permit process: If a firm has no permits experience with your local permits department, they should be penalized accordingly and to a level that best represents their level of direct face-to-face experience with the local permit officials. Not knowing the permit protocol for your jurisdiction can severely impact the project schedule.

SCORE, RANK, AND RECOMMEND
SHORT-LISTED FIRMS

Assigning a score is required in order to rank select sellers/firms so that a short list can be developed. Using all the evaluators' separate score sheets, the purchasing manager develops a detailed ranking list based on combining all the evaluators' scores. The top five firms are then identified and contacted to participate in the RFP process. Points scoring for criteria 1 through 9 above are based on a total of 100 points.

Criterion A:
- 10 points—firm experience
- 25 points—professional qualifications
- 10 points—most recent projects
- 25 points—most similar projects

Criterion B:
* 10 points—Ability to execute work (5 most recent projects), on time
* 10 points—Ability to execute work (5 most similar projects), on time

Criterion C:
* 10 points—Local knowledge and knowledge of the permit process

All of the evaluators will have different comments or issues. Following a recommended guide for evaluating firms, as outlined below, will help provide some consistency in scores. It is important to note that even with some consistency among evaluators, the evaluators may end up with numbers that are very different. For example, you may score a design firm a 10 on a particular criterion and another evaluator may give the same design firm a score of 5. In some cases the committee may want to have an evaluator provide a reason for such a difference in scores. Sometimes evaluators may interpret something differently or could be missing a page of the submitted information. The following is the order used when evaluating a design firm:

* Note any formatting errors.
* Note the staffing size of the primary firm. The design firm size will give insight regarding the capability of the firm. For example, if a firm has one architect located at the firm's local office and 10 located in another country, only count the one architect as part of the staff.
* Assign 2 points out of 10 for every project that fits your project exactly. For instance, if we use our example project from figure 1.1 and your project is a fire station, and the firm lists three of the five recently completed projects as fire stations, I would assign that firm 6 points.
* Assign 5 points out of 25 for every most similar project, past or present, which fits your project exactly. So if a firm lists five fire stations, using our example above, then I would assign 25 points.
* Assign 2 points out of 10 for every past project completed on time and on budget. If the five past projects are within the time and budget constraints, I would assign 10 points.
* Assign 2 points out of 10 for every most similar project completed on time and on budget. The same applies here as shown above. If all five projects are on time and budget, I would assign 10 points.
* Assign 5 points out of 10 for local knowledge. If a firm is located in the same county as the project, I assign 5 points, and an additional 5 points for detailed information related to our permit process. So if a firm is local I assign 5 points and if the firm has limited knowledge of the permitting

process I would only assign 3 points. Some firms will try to use their subconsultants' local experience. In many cases, design firms will use a local civil subconsultant but that only indicates that they are familiar with the site plan permitting process, and not the building permit process.

It is very important to explain your scoring philosophy for each firm by providing notes describing why they did not earn the maximum points. It will help the purchasing manager debrief the firms that did not make the short list.

Because you may have 20 to 30 firms to score, your team of evaluators will need to combine their scores in order to average the overall scores in determining the natural break point for choosing the top firms. For instance, you may end up with a separation of only 5 points between the top five firms and the sixth may have a separation of 7 points. This is a natural break point that will dictate a cut-off point for those firms that will make the short list.

Using our sample project outlined in figure 1.1 we would combine each reviewer's score for each criterion (A, B, and C) to develop a short list, using figure 2.2, firm #1, criterion A. The math used for calculating the average for each criterion is as follows:

$$\text{Composite score} \div \text{average (avg)} = 7.5$$
$$\text{Evaluator's scores} = (10 + 10 + 5 + 5) \div 4 = 7.5$$

Figure 2.3 shows a spreadsheet-based ranking that will help the review team determine the short list. Figure 2.4 shows the firms' rankings from the lowest score to the highest, left to right, and marks a logical break point.

DEBRIEFING DESIGN FIRMS

After the short list is established, the unsuccessful design firms need to be debriefed by the purchasing manager or the PM upon a firm's written request submitted within a reasonable time. The person conducting debriefings needs to be able to discuss the rationale for the selection decision and contract award. The debriefing needs to be limited to the design firm's own proposal and not those of competing design firms. Be factual and consistent; provide information on areas in which the design firm's proposal shows weakness or deficiencies. A debriefing should not include discussions or dissemination of the thoughts, notes, or rankings of evaluators, but a summary of the rationale for the selection decision and the recommended contract award can be discussed with the design firm.

Project Name: Anytown Fire Company #1 Fire Station Date: (Insert date)	Evalator	design firm 1	design firm 2	design firm 3	design firm 4	design firm 5	design firm 6	design firm 7	design firm 8	design firm 9	design firm 10	design firm 11	design firm 12	design firm 13	design firm 14	design firm 15	design firm 16	design firm 17	design firm 18	design firm 19	design firm 20
Criterion A: Firm experience and past performance on similar projects- 10 points	e1	10	10	10	10	10	10	10	10	10	10	10	10	10	10	10	10	10	10	10	10
	e2	10	10	10	10	10	10	10	10	10	10	10	10	10	10	10	10	10	10	10	10
	e3	5	6	10	5	9	8	8	9	9	6	5	6	6	7	7	7	0	2	2	1
	e4	5	5	10	8	8	10	10	5	5	5	5	5	2	5	2	1	4	5	6	5
	av	8	8	10	8	9	10	10	9	9	8	8	8	7	8	7	7	6	7	7	7
professional qualifications- 25 points	e1	23	25	22	25	25	25	20	21	19	15	20	25	25	25	8	25	25	25	25	25
	e2	25	25	25	24	25	25	18	22	21	23	22	22	25	12	25	25	25	15	23	22
	e3	15	16	12	15	21	20	12	15	17	18	23	11	13	18	18	23	12	20	22	22
	e4	19	25	25	15	25	20	15	17	20	18	20	15	14	20	20	20	19	15	20	25
	av	21	23	21	20	24	23	16	19	19	19	21	18	19	19	18	23	20	19	23	24
5- most recent projects- 10 points	e1	2	10	0	2	10	10	10	10	0	2	2	0	0	10	0	10	6	2	2	4
	e2	8	6	0	2	10	10	6	6	6	2	6	5	10	10	6	8	6	6	8	8
	e3	5	10	2	4	10	10	4	4	6	6	4	8	10	10	8	8	6	6	6	8
	e4	7	8	2	6	10	10	4	2	4	2	2	5	8	8	6	4	8	8	6	4
	av	6	9	1	4	10	10	6	6	4	3	4	5	7	10	5	8	7	6	6	6
5- most similar projects- 10 points	e1	10	8	8	6	2	4	2	4	2	4	8	10	8	10	10	10	2	2	6	10
	e2	10	10	8	4	6	6	4	4	4	2	6	10	8	8	10	8	2	6	10	10
	e3	10	4	8	8	8	8	4	8	8	8	8	10	8	6	10	6	2	4	8	8
	e4	10	10	8	8	4	8	4	8	4	8	8	10	6	10	10	8	4	4	8	6
	av	10	8	8	7	5	7	4	6	5	6	8	10	8	9	10	8	3	4	8	9
ability to execute work 5- most recent projects- 10 points	e1	10	10	4	4	10	4	6	6	6	10	8	6	4	4	6	2	4	2	6	8
	e2	10	8	5	8	10	6	2	2	6	10	8	2	4	8	6	0	6	6	8	6
	e3	8	6	4	8	8	8	8	2	4	8	8	2	2	8	10	2	6	6	6	4
	e4	6	4	4	4	4	6	4	6	4	8	10	8	6	8	8	6	8	6	6	4
	av	9	7	4	6	8	6	6	4	5	9	9	5	4	7	8	3	6	6	7	6
ability to execute work 5- most similar projects- 10 points	e1	10	8	5	8	10	6	2	2	6	10	8	2	6	8	6	0	6	6	8	6
	e2	8	6	4	8	8	8	8	2	4	8	8	2	6	8	10	2	6	6	6	4
	e3	6	8	4	4	4	4	6	6	4	8	10	8	6	8	8	6	8	6	6	4
	e4	10	8	8	6	2	4	2	4	2	4	8	10	8	10	10	10	2	2	6	10
	av	9	8	5	7	6	6	5	4	4	8	9	6	7	9	9	5	6	6	7	6
Local Knowledge- 10 points	e1	5	10	10	5	5	5	5	10	10	5	10	5	0	0	0	0	5	0	10	5
	e2	5	10	5	5	5	0	5	5	10	5	10	5	0	0	5	0	5	0	10	5
	e3	5	10	10	5	5	0	5	5	10	5	10	5	5	5	0	0	5	5	10	5
	e4	5	5	5	5	5	10	5	5	10	5	10	5	5	5	0	5	5	5	10	5
	av	5	9	0	5	5	4	5	6	10	5	10	5	3	4	0	1	5	3	10	5
totals	e1	70	81	59	60	72	64	55	63	53	56	66	58	53	67	40	57	58	47	67	68
	e2	76	75	57	61	74	65	53	51	61	60	70	56	63	61	67	53	60	49	75	65
	e3	54	60	50	49	65	58	47	49	58	59	68	50	50	62	61	52	39	51	60	52
	e4	62	65	62	52	58	66	46	47	49	50	63	58	49	66	56	54	50	47	62	59
	av	66	70	57	56	67	63	50	53	55	56	67	56	54	64	56	54	52	49	66	61

Figure 2.3

Project Name: Independent Fire Company #1 Fire Station Date: September 20, 2010	Evaluators	design firm 18	design firm 7	design firm 17	design firm 8	design firm 13	design firm 16	design firm 9	design firm 4	design firm 12	design firm 15	design firm 10	design firm 3	design firm 20	design firm 6	design firm 14	design firm 19	design firm 1	design firm 11	design firm 5	design firm 2
Criterion A: Firm experience and past performance on similar projects- 10 points	e1	10	10	10	10	10	10	10	10	10	10	10	10	10	10	10	10	10	10	10	10
	e2	10	10	10	10	10	10	10	10	10	10	10	10	10	10	10	10	10	10	10	10
	e3	2	8	0	9	6	7	9	5	6	7	6	10	1	8	7	2	5	5	9	6
	e4	5	10	4	5	2	1	5	8	5	2	5	10	5	10	5	6	5	5	8	5
	av	6.8	9.5	6	8.5	7	7	8.5	8.3	7.8	7.3	7.8	10	6.5	9.5	8	7	7.5	7.5	9.3	7.8
professional qualifications- 25 points	e1	25	20	25	21	25	25	19	25	25	8	15	22	25	25	25	25	23	20	25	25
	e2	15	18	25	22	25	25	21	24	22	25	23	25	22	25	12	23	25	22	25	25
	e3	20	12	12	15	13	23	17	15	11	18	18	12	22	20	18	22	15	23	21	16
	e4	15	15	19	17	14	20	20	15	15	20	18	25	25	20	20	20	19	20	25	23
	av	19	16	20	19	19	23	19	20	18	18	19	21	24	23	19	23	21	21	24	23
5- most recent projects- 10 points	e1	2	10	6	10	0	10	0	2	0	0	2	0	4	10	10	2	2	2	10	10
	e2	6	6	6	6	10	8	6	2	5	6	2	0	8	10	10	8	8	6	10	6
	e3	6	4	6	4	10	8	6	4	8	8	6	2	8	10	10	6	5	4	10	10
	e4	8	4	8	2	8	4	4	6	5	6	2	2	4	10	8	6	7	2	10	8
	av	5.5	6	6.5	5.5	7	7.5	4	3.5	4.5	5	3	1	6	10	9.5	5.5	5.5	3.5	10	8.5
5- most similar projects- 10 points	e1	2	2	2	4	8	10	2	6	10	10	4	8	10	4	10	6	10	8	2	8
	e2	6	4	2	4	8	8	4	4	10	10	2	8	10	6	8	10	10	6	6	10
	e3	4	4	2	8	8	6	8	8	10	10	8	8	8	6	8	10	8	4	8	4
	e4	4	4	4	8	6	8	4	8	10	10	8	8	6	8	10	8	10	8	4	10
	av	4	3.5	2.5	6	7.5	8	4.5	6.5	10	10	5.5	8	8.5	6.5	8.5	8	10	7.5	5	8
ability to execute work 5- most recent projects- 10 points	e1	2	6	4	6	4	2	6	4	6	6	10	4	8	4	4	6	10	8	10	10
	e2	6	2	6	2	4	0	6	8	2	6	10	5	6	6	8	8	10	8	10	8
	e3	6	8	6	2	2	2	4	8	2	10	8	4	4	8	8	6	10	8	8	6
	e4	8	6	8	6	6	6	4	4	8	8	8	4	4	4	8	6	10	10	4	4
	av	5.5	5.5	6	4	4	2.5	5	6	4.5	7.5	9	4.3	5.5	5.5	7	6.5	10	8.5	8	7
ability to execute work 5- most similar projects- 10 points	e1	6	2	6	2	6	0	6	8	2	6	10	5	6	6	8	8	8	8	10	8
	e2	6	8	6	2	6	2	4	8	2	10	4	4	8	4	4	8	8	8	8	6
	e3	8	6	8	6	6	6	4	4	8	8	4	4	4	8	6	8	10	4	8	8
	e4	2	2	2	4	8	10	2	6	10	10	4	8	2	4	10	6	8	8	2	8
	av	5.5	4.5	5.5	3.5	6.5	4.5	4	6.5	5.5	8.5	7.5	5.3	4	5.5	8.5	6.5	8	8.5	6	7.5
Local Knowledge- 10 points	e1	0	5	5	10	0	0	10	5	5	0	5	10	5	5	0	10	5	10	5	10
	e2	0	5	5	5	0	0	10	5	5	0	5	5	5	0	5	10	5	10	5	10
	e3	5	5	5	5	5	0	10	5	5	0	5	10	5	0	5	10	5	10	5	10
	e4	5	5	5	5	5	5	10	5	5	0	5	5	5	5	5	10	5	10	5	10
	av	2.5	5	5	6.3	2.5	1.3	10	5	5	0	5	0	5	3.8	3.8	10	5	10	5	10
Total	e1	47	55	58	63	53	57	53	60	58	40	56	59	68	64	67	67	68	66	72	81
	e2	49	53	60	51	63	53	61	61	56	67	60	57	65	65	61	75	76	70	74	75
	e3	51	47	39	49	50	52	58	49	50	61	59	50	52	58	62	60	58	68	65	60
	e4	47	46	50	47	49	54	49	52	58	56	50	62	51	66	66	62	64	63	58	70
rank	av	49	50	52	53	54	54	55	56	56	56	56	57	59	63	64	66	67	67	67	72

logical break point

Figure 2.4

3

Request for Proposal (RFP) Short List Bidding and Awarding Services

RFP DEVELOPMENT

After meeting with the evaluators and purchasing manager, the project manager will have agreed on the top firms that will move on to the RFP (see appendix B) stage of award, based on final scoring of the short-listed firms using composite scores. It is the end of the long-list process and the beginning of the RFP process.

During RFP evaluation, each schedule activity/task is assigned a score depending on what is more important to the organization. Assigning 30 possible points for a technical proposal, 40 possible points for an interview, and 30 points for a fee proposal represents a standard scoring structure. Working with the purchasing manager, evaluators can assign possible points based on what is important to the organization. For instance, you may want to apply more points to the fee proposal and reduce the technical/interview proposal points. In place of a 70/30 split in points, with 70 being the technical/interview score and 30 being the fee score, you may want a 75/25 split if technical proficiency is more important, or a 60/40 split if cost is more important. Remember the saying "you only get what you pay for" when assigning possible points; the goal is not to hire the cheapest firm but the best value, that is, the most qualified firm at competitive prices.

The following is a checklist of items that should be included in an RFP:

☐ Cover page: Include the organization's logo to help identify the document.
☐ RFP number: Numbers are typically assigned by purchasing to keep track of projects in the organization.

☐ Proposal due date: The date RFPs need to be submitted to purchasing for intake and distribution to the interview/evaluation team.

☐ Preproposal date: A preproposal conference allows the firms an opportunity to ask questions and perform a site visit if they wish.

☐ Table of contents: Outlines all the content of the RFP and identifies page numbers of each section.

☐ Project overview: Includes a brief overview of the need for the project and a summary of the required design work, including a description of required subconsultants.

☐ Scope of services: Provides a detailed narrative of services including all the requirements for design.

☐ Description of technical and fee proposal system: Informs the design firms how the system is divided into points for scoring and describes the criteria.

☐ Proposal terms and conditions: Describes and informs the design firms of organizational rules regarding the detailed process of an RFP and what rules the firms will need to adhere to if hired.

☐ Instruction for submitting proposals: Details how a firm must submit their documentation to purchasing in order to qualify for an RFP review.

☐ Proposal form: Fees are outlined on this page and submitted in the second stage of the RFP process.

☐ Non-collusion certification: This form is signed by the authorized individual of the firm indicating that no members of the firm are associated with the project.

☐ Affirmative action data form: This is an equal opportunity form that must be filled out by the firm in order to participate in the RFP process. It is used so that minority businesses, small businesses, and women-owned businesses can participate.

☐ Joint venture eligibility: If two firms are combining to partner on one individual project, they will need to provide this information.

☐ Technical proposal evaluation form: This is a copy of the form used by the evaluators to score the firms on the technical portion of the proposal, provided so firms can see what will be evaluated.

☐ Interview evaluation form: This is used to score the firms after the interviews. Structured questions developed and agreed to by the interviewers and purchasing manager are needed prior to interviewing the firms. It is important to ask each firm these structured questions so that scoring can be more consistent. These questions are not to be provided to the design firm before the interview.

☐ Project hours summary: Under the fee proposal stage, the firms will supply a breakdown of hours for their work and their subconsultants' work.

☐ Fee proposal summary: Similar to a project hours summary but is a break-down of costs for the firm and each subconsultant.

☐ Hourly rate schedule: Billable hourly rates, which are entered into a schedule of values in order to generate pay requisitions based on the ac-tual work provided up to a certain date, indicating the cost of each firm's staff members associated with your project.

☐ Program requirements: Provides a predesign concept plan and/or program with details such as how the total square footage required for the project is divided into individual spaces by square footage.

☐ Geotechnical study: Required if you need to know the ground you are building on will support the structure and provides recommendations to correct any soil conditions, if needed, before starting the RFP process. Or-ganizations may have geotechnical information on a prospective property. If not, the PM may need to obtain one through an RFQ process. Providing a geotechnical report as part of the RFP invitation will allow design firms to better prepare for any abnormal civil engineering requirements.

☐ Archeological study: A phase I study may be required in order to get a permit to build on land that may have some historical significance. Ad-ditionally, a phase II or phase III study may be required based on the findings of the phase I study. If this occurs, you may need to find another building location.

ESTABLISHING A DESIGN TIMELINE

In order for potential design firms to provide a more realistic and accurate schedule of deliverables, schedule development needs to be based on assump-tions about the length of review times, which are based on schedule manage-ment plans and related to permit processes. I have found that just about every jurisdiction is different when determining review time frames, so I developed the schedule shown in figure 3.1 as a base line. It is important to provide some sort of preliminary schedule so that design firms can submit an accurate fee proposal, but the goal is to have the design firm provide a recommended schedule so you can determine if they have included all the tasks that you've identified as crucial to project success. Design firms need to give owners de-tailed schedule information and milestone data, based on a master schedule, and related to the design sequence of a project with enough lead time to allow the schedule to be updated when needed.

Detailed information furnished by the awarded design firm needs to allow a minimum of two weeks for the organization's review of each interim design submission and a minimum of three weeks for the review of the final 95% CD design submission. The design firm also must allow review time for submittals to authorities having jurisdiction over the project, and allow time for at least one iteration for each submission. The design firm will need to inform the owner about design progress in relation to target dates, and must control the design progress and staffing of the design firm to meet the project target dates. Review of this projected progress schedule must be submitted to the PM for approval in a timely manner.

Figure 3.1.1 shows an organization's proposed bar chart, also known as a Gannt chart. Gannt charts illustrate the start and finish dates of milestones and activities that are required to complete a project. Additionally, the chart is used to show a project's proposed activity start and end dates, along with the proposed number of days needed to perform tasks, which is a way to reveal the critical path of a project.

In order to track activities based on a submitted schedule and a schedule model, PMs may employ a precedence diagramming method (PDM) for sequencing activities. Also referred to as the activity on node (AON) method, as opposed to activity on arrow (AOA), it uses nodes depicted as boxes or rectangles connected by arrows in a manner that will eventually identify a project's critical path. Using a precedence network, the PM can develop the precedence relationships using predecessor and successor activities.

CRITICAL PATH METHOD (CPM)

The critical path method (CPM) is used to calculate the longest path of a project schedule by establishing an information box representing pertinent scheduling information based on early start and finish dates and late start and finish dates for all the scheduled activity/tasks needed to complete the project, from concept to final use. The technique for CPM is to construct a model for the project that includes all the project activities/tasks needed for project success, the number of days required for each task, and how the tasks relate to one another.[15]

Early and late start and finish dates will show the time periods in which a scheduled task should take place, given task times, logical relationships, leads, lags, and other evident constraints.

Tasks on a critical path are called critical tasks. Adjustments to task durations, logical relationships, leads and lags, or other schedule constraints may be necessary to produce network paths with a zero or positive total float. Once the total float for a network path is zero or positive, then the free float, that is, slack, which is the amount of time that the task can be delayed without delaying the early start date of any immediate successor task within the network path, can also be determined. By performing a forward pass computation and backward pass computation through the network paths, we can calculate early

Figure 3.1.1

Activity ID	Description	Orig Dur	Rem Dur	Early Start	Early Finish
1000	Total Project Time	373 *	373 *	13OCT09 *	23OCT10
1051	Design Start	0	0	13OCT09	
1060	35% design and submission	30	30	13OCT09	11NOV09
1061	35% Review and comment	21	21	12NOV09	02DEC09
1062	Site plan submission to planning after 35%	75	75	03DEC09 *	17FEB10
1070	50% Design and submission	30	30	03DEC09 *	03JAN10
1071	50% Review and comment	21	21	04JAN10 *	24JAN10
1090	95% Desgin phase	50	50	25JAN10 *	15MAR10
1095	95% Review and comment	21	21	16MAR10	05APR10
1100	Building permit submission with 95%	75	75	06APR10 *	19JUN10
1110	Bid set preperation for advertisement	10	10	20JUN10 *	29JUN10
1111	Add date	15	15	30JUN10	15JUL10
1112	Pre-Bid	0	0	16JUL10 *	
1113	RFI Review and comment	30	30	16JUL10 *	14AUG10
1114	Bid opening	0	0		14AUG10 *
1120	Prepare and route award recomendation	15	15	15AUG10	29AUG10
1130	Recomendation for award to Purchasing	15	15	30AUG10	13SEP10
1140	Route Contracts	15	15	14SEP10 *	28SEP10
1151	Pre-construcition meeting set by DCMI	15	15	29SEP10	13OCT10
1160	Construction start	10	10	14OCT10	23OCT10

OPM
Design Phasing

Start date	13OCT09
Finish date	23OCT10
Data date	13OCT09
Run date	26JAN11
Page number	1A

© Primavera Systems, Inc.

Legend:
- ▭ Early bar
- ▭ Progress bar
- ▭ Critical bar
- ▭ Summary bar
- ◇ Start milestone point
- ◇ Finish milestone point

and late start and finish dates. Since many examples are available, I will not be performing a forward and backward pass exercise here, but the formulas are as follows:

ES = Early Start
EF = Early Finish
LF = Late Finish
LS = Late Start
Forward Pass:
ES = EF of the predecessor task
EF = ES + the task duration
Backward Pass:
LF = LS of the successor task
LS = LF – the task duration

It is important to know that once paths are identified, the PM can then see what activities are on the critical path, identifying path convergence or path divergence, and those activities that can be delayed before they start to impact the critical path. Float, or slack, can then be assigned for noncritical tasks and a time assigned based on the last day the item becomes critical. This can be seen once an activity no longer runs parallel to the critical path. Remember that the critical path does not include any float. If a project's critical path is too long, PMs will try to shorten it by fast-tracking or crashing the schedule. Known as schedule compression, crashing allows for a time reduction to complete a task on the critical path by adding resources, which can result in increases of cost. Fast-tracking is another schedule compression technique in which tasks that are typically performed successively are now being performed concurrently. This can increase a project's risk, due to work being performed without completely vetted information.

The following formulas are used to calculate slack and free float:

$$\text{Slack time} = LF - EF + LS - ES$$
$$\text{Free Float} = ES \text{ (successor task)} - EF \text{ (predecessor task)}$$

PROGRAM EVALUATION AND
REVIEW TECHNIQUE (PERT)

Figure 3.1.2 is an example of what results are generated by using a program evaluation and review technique (PERT) method, that is, a three-point estimate for developing a project schedule network diagram.

Figure: Primavera schedule network diagram — "OPM Design Phasing"

ID	TF	Description	OD	ES	EF	LS	LF
1000	0	Total Project Time	373 * / 373 *	13OCT09	23OCT10	13OCT09	23OCT10
1051	0	Design Start	0 / 0	13OCT09		13OCT09	
1060	0	35% design and	30 / 30	13OCT09	11NOV09	13OCT09	11NOV09
1061	0	35% Review and comment	21 / 21	12NOV09	02DEC09	12NOV09	02DEC09
1062	47d	Site plan submission to	75 / 75	03DEC09	17FEB10	21JAN10	05APR10
1070	0	50% Design and	30 / 30	03DEC09	03JAN10	03DEC09	03JAN10
1071	0	50% Review and comment	21 / 21	04JAN10 *	24JAN10	04JAN10	24JAN10
1090	0	95% Desgin phase	50 / 50	25JAN10 *	15MAR10	25JAN10	15MAR10
1095	0	95% Review and comment	21 / 21	16MAR10	05APR10	16MAR10	05APR10
1100	0	Building permit	75 / 75	06APR10	19JUN10	06APR10	19JUN10
1110	0	Bid set preparation	10 / 10	20JUN10	29JUN10	20JUN10	29JUN10
1111	0	Add date	15 / 15	30JUN10	15JUL10	30JUN10	15JUL10
1112	0	Pre-Bid	0 / 0	16JUL10 *		16JUL10	
1113	30	RFI Review and comment	30 / 30	16JUL10 *	14AUG10	16JUL10	14AUG10
1114	0	Bid opening	0 / 0	14AUG10		14AUG10	
1120	0	Prepare and route award	15 / 15	15AUG10	29AUG10	15AUG10	29AUG10
1130	0	Recomendatic for award to	15 / 15	30AUG10	13SEP10	30AUG10	13SEP10
1140	15	Route Contracts	15 / 15	14SEP10	28SEP10	14SEP10	28SEP10
1151	0	Pre-construct meeting set	15 / 15	29SEP10	13OCT10	29SEP10	13OCT10
1160	0	Construction start	10 / 10	14OCT10	23OCT10	14OCT10	23OCT10

Start date 13OCT09
Finish date 23OCT10
Data date 13OCT09
Run date 28SEP11
Page number 1A

OPM
Design Phasing

© Primavera Systems, Inc.

Legend:
ACT	TF
DESC	OD
ES	EF	RD
LS	LF	

— Driving relationship
--- Nondriving relationship
■ Critical color

Figure 3.1.2

PERT allows for the assignment of activities required to complete a given project, especially the time needed to complete each activity, and identifies the minimum time needed to complete a project. Once the activities have been developed, the PM can then use a CPM to find the critical path, which is the longest path through a project schedule represented by activities that cannot be delayed without delaying the finish date. The PM can then fast-track, if required by the organization, the project by determining which activities can be done concurrently without affecting the critical path. Keep in mind that a schedule may have more than one critical path, thus increasing the risk of a delay.

It is important to note that PERT is a good method to determine unknown durations for activities if an estimate of time is not evident, due to lack of experience or not having a project history of similar tasks and their actual durations.

To find an unknown duration the PM will need input from others. This is done by gathering three durations from other PMs, subject matter experts (SMEs), or your supervisors, and calculating the results. For example, you have an activity that you are guessing might take 14 days to accomplish; this is considered the most pessimistic time to complete the task—the most pessimistic time will always be the longest duration guessed. Your boss may be more optimistic, with a recommended duration of eight days. Then you talk to another PM who has done this activity on a past project and find that they would recommend a most likely duration of 10 days. Using the above guesses and the following formula, you can calculate the expected activity duration:

$$\text{pessimistic} + (4 \times \text{most likely}) + \text{optimistic} \div 6$$
$$12 + (4 \times 10) + 8 \div 6 = 10$$
Expected activity duration is 10 days

Another method of obtaining expected task time is by employing benchmarking. It is a process that uses data available from a previous but similar project with the same scope of work and services. Using this past project activity duration, you can use this number as the most likely duration and plug it into the formula above to find the expected activity duration.

Let's say you still are not certain that 10 days is the best guess and would like a little bit more assurance. You can then calculate a standard deviation and apply it to whatever percentage of how correct you feel this number to be. The formula is as follows:

$$\text{Standard deviation } (\sigma) = (\text{pessimistic} - \text{optimistic}) \div 6$$
$$(12 - 8) \div 6 = .67$$
$$\sigma = .67$$

So based on σ = .67 and using the following calculations, you can predict certainty expressed by a percent and then a range of days. For example, you may want to be 68.26% sure that the work is finished within ±1 standard deviation; 95.44% that represents finishing the work within ±2 standard deviations; and 99.73% which represents finished work ±3 standard deviations. This is known as the specification limits or control limits, and is shown graphically by a control chart. So the math looks like this, using the expected activity duration of 10 days:

- With 68.26% certainty your project activity will take 10 − .67 = 9.33 days, or 10 + .67 = 10.67 days. So with this percentage of certainty you can figure on this task taking between 9.33 and 10.67 days.
- With 95.44% certainty the activity will take 10 − (.67 × 2) = 8.66 days or 10 + (.67 × 2) = 11.34 days. So with this percentage of certainty you can figure on this task taking between 8.66 days and 11.34 days.
- With 99.73% certainty the activity will take 10 − (.67 × 3) = 7.99 days or 10 + (.67 × 3) = 12.01 days. So with this percentage of certainty you can figure on this task taking between 7.99 days and 12.01 days.

You may be wondering how I arrived at these percentages. Without providing a full lecture about how the equations are developed, I used what is known as the 68-95-99.7 rule, also known as the three-sigma rule, or the empirical rule. Knowing that the data distribution is approximately normal, then 68.26% of the data values are within one standard deviation of the mean, 95.44% are within two standard deviations, and 99.73% lie within three standard deviations, as shown in figure 3.1.3.[16] It is important to mention that even though three standard deviations work fine in determining schedule durations, in other industries more accuracy may be required; Six Sigma may be needed in order to achieve high levels of quality with few defects. At the Six Sigma level, accuracy is 99.99966%. For instance, if a manufacturer of car springs produces 1 million units, 3.4 of them will not pass quality standards and will be rejected. This means that most of the springs will fall within the manufacturer's quality limits.

SCOPE OF SERVICES

Because most organizations have an outline, such as an activity list with an activity identifier, of what they require from design firms already developed and in place based on past projects, PMs will utilize these previously developed scope of services and tailor them based on individual project needs. An

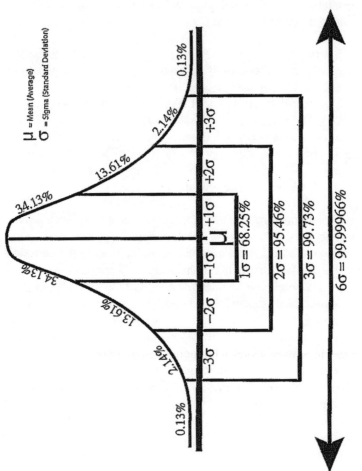

μ = Mean (Average)
σ = Sigma (Standard Deviation)

34.13%   34.13%
13.61%   13.61%
2.14%   2.14%
0.13%   0.13%

−3σ   −2σ   −1σ   μ   +1σ   +2σ   +3σ

1σ = 68.25%
2σ = 95.46%
3σ = 99.73%

6σ = 99.99966%

Figure 3.1.3

outline of a sample scope of services is included in the sample RFP (see appendix B). In the event that an organization has not developed any scope of services in the past, the PM will need to develop an outline for the services required.

When developing a scope of services, PMs may start by first developing a work breakdown structure (WBS). This is a tool used to help develop and identify a framework of overall activities, which will be planned and controlled by breaking them up into manageable work packages to reveal all the steps required to complete a project. Once all the tasks have been identified, a PM will then implement the PERT method to identify all major tasks, subtasks, and components. Using the PERT information, a PM can then identify the critical path of the project. If the organization wants to fast-track the project, the PM can simply identify the tasks that can be done concurrently to shorten the critical path. And later if the organization wants to crash the schedule, the PM can identify where additional resources can be used to shorten the critical path.

RFP DISTRIBUTION

When distributing an RFP to firms, the PM also needs to submit copies to evaluators. Once firms respond by sending their proposals to the purchasing manager, copies are made and distributed to evaluators. Keep in mind that the purchasing manager will only distribute the first part of the overall RFP, with the technical evaluation and interview making up the first part. The fee proposal is the second part. The fee proposal is never given to the evaluation team until the technical and interview portions of the RFP are scored. This allows evaluators to provide scores without the bias of a fee.

TECHNICAL PROPOSAL REQUIREMENTS

Adhering to the format is essential in order for firms to score well. No additional materials, such as brochures, should be included, due to time constraints. The responses to technical portions of the proposal are evaluated and ranked based on the information gathered on the technical evaluation form (see the sample RFP for the sample technical evaluation form). All technical submissions under the RFP should include the following:

1. A brief description of the firm's history and organization. This section should also include an organizational chart of key personnel assigned to

the project, including consultants. Resumes must be included and must be limited to individuals who will actually be assigned to and working on the project, with each individual resume limited to a maximum of one page.

2. Five recent projects in the past three years, with each project description limited to a maximum of two pages. Projects by subconsultants that the design firm feels are beneficial and applicable to the project should be included among the five projects. Photographs of example projects are strongly encouraged. If color photographs are being submitted, they should be included in each copy of the RFP. The firm will also need to include the owner's representative's contact numbers (phone and fax).

3. The firm needs to individually and specifically address the following criteria in the order indicated:

    a. The firm's availability and ability to commit the necessary staff and resources to accomplish the project.

    b. The firm's method for project budgeting and cost estimating, and specific results.

    c. The firm's methods for quality control of construction documents and specific results.

    d. Any other additional information not requested above that the firm feels may be useful and applicable to the project.

4. A project hours summary sheet is needed to indicate the estimated man-hours required to complete a project. The projected man-hours need to be broken down by design phase for each design discipline associated with a project. The project hours summary sheet is submitted as part of the technical proposal and included in the technical proposal envelope submitted to the purchasing manager.

ORGANIZATIONAL CHART

Organizational charts show the relationships between all the key players involved in a typical project. The charts are developed in various formats to identify the project team and team responsibilities. Figure 3.2 is an organization breakdown structure (OBS) chart, a hierarchical chart with a typical layout that identifies positions and relationships graphically.

RFP SCORING CRITERIA

Scoring criteria is outlined in the RFP so that the design firms can assemble their proposal according to the directions. Deciding what the important needs

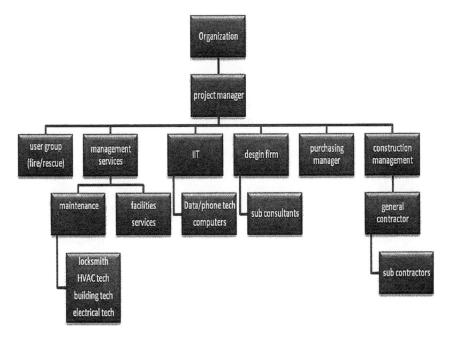

Figure 3.2

of a project are, and tailoring them into criteria, are the responsibility of the PM and the purchasing manager. Although similar to the SOQ long list criteria, the difference is that firms will be required to expand on their SOQ criteria, and assigned points are more detailed. Evaluation criteria may include the following with possible points assigned:

Firm experience and past performance on similar projects: 35 total points

1. Identify firm name, address, telephone, type of ownership   2
2. Provide firm history, organizational charts   2
3. Identify personnel with ability to commit firm to this project   2
4. Identify insurance policies carried by firm   2
5. Describe firm's experience in providing similar services   6
6. Give firm's size, including number of technical and support staff 2
7. List five projects completed in the past three years and identify the following:
   a. Project name   1
   b. Project location   1

c.	Description of scope of services	5
d.	Name of owner	1
e.	Name and telephone number of owner's contact person	1
f.	Members of the project team	2
g.	Role played by each member	2
h.	Cost control measures, include change order information	2
i.	Measures used to keep timelines and level of success	2

8. Identify if the firm has utilized standard construction front-end documents formulated by AIA or EJCDC. 2

Professional qualifications for performance of required services:

35 total points

1. Describe team structure and project principals proposed to manage the team 5
2. Identify the project manager 3
3. Identify the architect/interior designer 3
4. Identify the civil engineer 3
5. Identify the structural engineer 3
6. Identify the mechanical engineer 3
7. Identify the electrical engineer 3
8. Identify the geotechnical engineer 3
9. Identify the surveyor 3
10. Identify the fire protection engineer 3
11. Identify the independent third-party professional cost estimator 3

Demonstrated capacity to do the work in the required time: 20 total points

1. List firm's current projects or commitments and their percentage of completion 9
2. List firm's current commitments for the professional staff identified to work on the project 7
3. Provide information that will indicate firm's ability to provide services with little advance notice and very tight schedules 4

Local knowledge: 10 total points

1. Identify firm's familiarity with the local geographic area 3
2. Identify firm's familiarity with local permitting rules and regulations 4
3. Describe firm's familiarity with local construction firms and local subcontractors that would likely bid on the project 3

REVIEW AND RESPOND TO REQUESTS
FOR INFORMATION (RFIS)

Rarely during an RFP do requests for information (RFIs) get submitted, but occasionally a question may come up. Most questions will be presented during a pre-bid meeting. All those questions will be gathered and answered via addenda. After the meeting and seven days before the due date, RFIs will be accepted but need to be submitted in writing to the purchasing manager and passed on to the PM for responses to questions. The purchasing manger will then compile the questions and responses and publish an addendum. Any addenda will supersede that section of the original RFP. How you answer the questions is very important in maintaining clear responses. Answers need to follow the same order and format of the RFP in order to avoid confusion.

RFP VERSUS QBS

In deciding how your organization selects a design firm two methods can be employed, an RFP or a qualifications-based selection (QBS) process. RFPs are similar to SOQs, but more detailed in that they require a fee proposal before a contract is awarded to the design firm. When determining which method to use, some questions will need to be answered. For example, if your organization is more interested in cost and satisfactory quality, an RFP process could be used, but if superior quality and possibly paying more for this are desired, QBS can be employed.

Developing a QBS starts when the organization identifies the need for a project and develops a well-defined scope of work so that the interested design firms can submit their RFQ or SOQ tailored to project requirements as advertised by the purchasing department. Starting with a well-defined scope of work, the design firms will generate qualifications and submit them in accordance with the instructions. Following the SOQ process, a short list of firms is developed and recommended for approval by the organization.[17] Selected firms are contacted and sent information regarding the next step in the QBS process as follows:

1. A pre-interview date is established. A site visit or building tour will be included as part of the meeting. This will help firms get a look at all the existing conditions and address any immediate concerns or questions. After this meeting, RFIs might be generated and answered before submittals are due.

2. The purchasing manager will send each firm a packet of instructions includ-
    ing any responses to RFIs, due date of submittals, instructions regarding
    the scoring and selection process, and how evaluators will be conducting
    interviews. Also included is any information the organization may have
    such as feasibility studies, an existing program, and any site studies.

After the short-listed firms have had ample time to review and submit information, the procurement manager will distribute the information to the
evaluators for review. Concurrently, interview dates, agreed to by the PM
and procurement manager, will be sent out to short-listed firms. Evaluators
are important in the QBS process because it allows the organization an opportunity to hear different ideas and approaches regarding the design for your
project and will help reveal the firms' understanding of the project. It allows
individual styles for each firm to be evaluated along with their subconsultants.
The same interview steps employed under the RFP process can be used here.
If a firm does not have all the recommended subconsultants at the interview,
they should be penalized.

Once the firms have been ranked, the organization can then negotiate a price.
If the two parties cannot agree on price then the organization has the right to
move on to the next qualified firm and so on until agreement is reached.

INTERVIEW SHORT-LISTED FIRMS

Once the technical review is completed by the evaluation team and scores
turned over to the purchasing manager, evaluators will conduct interviews
with each prospective design firm. Each firm should be allowed 30 minutes to
present their qualifications, then 15–20 minutes for a structured question-and-
answer period where each firm will be asked to respond to the same three or
four questions. Questions may range from design techniques to project plans
of action. The evaluators will conclude with a final 10–15 minute free exchange of questions and presentation of additional information the firm feels
may be beneficial and applicable to the project. Personnel representing the
design firm shall be limited to individuals who will be actually assigned and
working on the project. The order of the interviews needs to be determined
by a straw poll. Responses to the interview will be evaluated and ranked in
accordance with the evaluation form. There should be no references or conversations regarding the firm's fee proposal during the interview.

An interview evaluation form, found in the sample RFP, will be needed to
gather all the evaluator's data on each firm. Various topics to listen for during
the interview might include the following:

- Related project experience
- Ability and capacity to perform the work
- A complete grasp of the project requirements
- Descriptions of the firm's management approach to technical requirements
- Detailed knowledge of the design process and methodologies that need to be applied to your project

Establishing points for categories that are of interest to your organization's project success need to be assigned. For example, using the information from figure 1.1 we can assign these general categories and assign points to them as follows:

1. Design firms' presentation and possible points assigned if they address any of the following (1 point each up to a total of 5 points):
   a. General discussion of the firm's organization
   b. Updated project experience
   c. Discussions regarding the programmed spaces
   d. Design approach discussion
   e. Propose a design with reasonable expectations regarding cost
   f. Design focused on timeline
   g. Subconsultant introductions and their roles in the project
   h. Responsiveness to issues during construction
   i. Discussions regarding site analysis
2. Analysis of structured questions. Depending on the project you may ask the following questions. Pick three to ask each firm and be sure to ask the question the same way for each firm (5 points):
   a. What is your firm's average response time to RFIs during construction?
   b. Would each subconsultant have a qualified person available on an as-needed basis to attend progress meetings and address directly any RFIs related to their services provided?
   c. Does your firm have an emergency contact for after-hour emergencies?
   d. Can you describe your firm's past experience with similar programs?
   e. Describe your experience with the permits office having jurisdiction to enforce codes and their processes?
   f. What types of project tracking software are you familiar with?
3. Analysis of subjective statements and closing remarks should be evaluated based on a free exchange of questions and answers among the evaluators and the design firm. Some things to look for when scoring are as follows (5 points):

a. Listen to their closing remarks and write down any questions you may have for them.
b. Listen to see if they have a real interest in working with your organization on the project.
c. Listen for responses that are vague.
d. Ask again if the personnel assigned to the project are licensed to practice in your state.
e. Note the design firm's mood to see if they seem enthusiastic about the project.

SCORE AND RANK FIRMS

Once design firms are interviewed and scored by each evaluator, combined scores are generated by the purchasing manager to rank design firms based on composite scores. Once the technical and interview portions are ranked, the evaluators then obtain fee proposals for scoring the second portion of the RFP from the purchasing manager. When the firms are developing their RFP submission documents, they are directed to submit the technical and fee portion in two separately sealed envelopes so that they can be evaluated independently.

FEE PROPOSAL AND EVALUATION

The fee for the project is based on a lump sum and includes any fees for allowances. Allowances are established to provide compensation to a firm for expenses such as geotechnical studies and renderings. Renderings will help illustrate the design concepts and can be used for marketing efforts, press releases, and presentations.

When firms submit their fee proposal for evaluation, they need to detail the costs and time for each subconsultant to perform their scope of work. This will later serve as the basis of payment similar to a contractor's schedule of values.

The fee proposal packet needs to include the information asked for per the directions in the RFP. If something is not provided, the purchasing manager will call the firm to see if they can provide it. If not, they will be disqualified. Packages should include the following:

1. Cover page:
   - A cover page indicating that the document is the firm's fee proposal for related design services

- Organization's bid number or project number assigned to identify the project
- Name of the project
- Date and time of the bid opening
- Firm's name and address along with work phone number

2. Fee proposal form:
   - Firm's name and address
   - Base bid price for services as defined in the RFP
   - Detail any additional alternates needed, showing the price separately from the base bid
   - Area for the firm's authorized representative to sign

3. Project hours summary: The design firms will indicate the estimated number of man-hours required to complete the project, broken down by design phase and by subconsultants associated with the work packages that will make up the overall SOW for the entire project.

4. Fee proposal summary: The design firms will indicate their fee and each subconsultant's fee to complete the project, broken down by design phase and by subconsultants' associated costs, by work packages that will make up the overall SOW for the entire project.

5. Hourly rate schedule: The design firms will indicate the hourly rate schedules for their staff and each subconsultant staff member associated with the project. This may include but not be limited to the following:
   - Principal
   - Project manager-senior
   - Draftsperson-project manager
   - Administrative/staff architect
   - Civil engineer/designer
   - Licensed surveyor
   - Surveyor crew
   - Senior cost estimator

6. Non-collusion certification: This form certifies that the firm has no personal affiliation to the organization; in my case it would be any county staff or board of directors associated with an organization doing business with the county.

7. Affirmative action data form: To ensure equal opportunity in project bidding, this will help monitor the effectiveness of the equal opportunity bidding.

When scoring the fee proposals, a system of averages based on price from high to low needs to be established. Using our information provided in the fee proposals and assuming we have short-listed five firms, we can use the following calculation to rank firms by price.

Based on a score of 25 points, we would assign the following:

25 points ÷ 5 firms = 5
25 points for the lowest price
20 points for second-lowest price
15 points for third-lowest price
10 points for fourth-lowest price
5 points for fifth-lowest price

After scores are collected by the purchasing manager, because the purchasing office is the gatekeeper for this task, the office will assemble a final scoring sheet with the following points assigned:

• 60 possible points for qualifications submitted per the directions of the RFP.
• 10 possible points for any updated information provided under the SOQ process and mentioning quality control/quality assurance methods, along with subconsultant relationships.
• 15 possible points for the interview.
• 25 possible points for the fee proposal.

If we use our sample project from figure 1.1 and use the form in figure 2.3 we can see that the short-listed firms might end up with the results shown in figure 3.3.

REVIEW REFERENCES

Once you have established rankings of the top firms, the evaluation team will assign each reviewer a firm to contact and verify their references. Firms should list owners they have recently worked for on their reference sheet and/ or any example projects in their proposal. The reference sheet should include:

1. Name of project
2. Brief description of work performed
3. The owner's name
4. The owner's contact person
5. Date of project completion
6. Contact numbers (phone and fax)
7. E-mail address

Project Name: Independent Fire Company #1 Fire Station Date: September 20, 2010	Evaluators/Interviewers	(5) design firm 19	(4) design firm 1	(3) design firm 11	(2) design firm 5	(1) design firm 2
qualifications submitted per the directions of the RFP (60 possible points)	e1	55	58	50	57	60
	e2	60	52	50	60	60
	e3	52	54	50	60	50
	e4	55	60	48	60	50
	ave	55.5	56	49.5	59.25	55
for any updated information provided under the SOQ process and mentioning quality control/quality assurance methods, along with sub-consultant relationships (10 possible points)	e1	8	6	8	8	10
	e2	8	8	10	5	10
	e3	8	6	10	10	8
	e4	8	5	8	10	8
	ave	8	6.25	9	8.25	9
for the interview (15 possible points)	e1	12	8	12	14	15
	e2	12	8	12	14	15
	e3	10	8	12	15	12
	e4	10	8	10	13	10
	ave	11	8	11.5	14	13
for the fee proposal (25 possible points)	e1	5	25	20	10	15
	e2	5	25	20	10	15
	e3	5	25	20	10	15
	e4	5	25	20	10	15
	ave	5	25	20	10	15
TOTAL	e1	80	97	90	89	100
	e2	85	93	92	89	100
	e3	75	93	92	95	85
	e4	78	98	86	93	83
	ave	79.5	95.25	90	91.5	92
Final Rank	e1	5	2	4	3	1
	e2	5	2	3	4	1
	e3	5	2	3	1	4
	e4	5	1	4	2	3
	ave	5	1.75	3.5	2.5	2.25
			winner			

Figure 3.3

8. Physical address
9. Position held by the contact person

Establishing contact with the references listed will be of great benefit when trying to evaluate the information that the firm provides. Barring any outrageously bad mistakes, we look at references to see if the firm made any mistakes or out-of-the-ordinary change orders to the original work, and also ask these questions:

1. Was this a favorable experience?
2. Was the design completed within budget and on schedule?

3. Were there unexpected difficulties during construction?
4. Could you describe their responsiveness? Did they provide timely and accurate responses to RFIs during construction?
5. Would you recommend them for future design projects?

RFP PROTEST

A design firm has the right to protest the award of a contract to the purchasing manager. The protest needs to be submitted in writing and addressed to the purchasing manager.

Protests based upon alleged improprieties in any type of bid solicitation that are apparent before proposal opening or closing date should be filed, meaning received by the purchasing office, before proposal opening or by the closing date and time for the receipt of proposals. In all other cases, proposal protests need to be filed within seven days after the basis for protest is known or should have been known, whichever is earlier. Any protest filed after that time limit will not be considered.

A written protest should include the following:

1. The name and address of the protestor
2. Appropriate identification of the procurement, and, if a contract has been awarded, its number
3. A statement of reasons for the protest
4. Supporting exhibits, evidence, or documents to substantiate any claims unless not available within the filing time, in which case the expected availability date shall be indicated

The purchasing manager will submit a copy of the protest to the legal department, or in my case a county attorney, upon receipt of the protest. Any additional information requested of the protestor by the purchasing manager needs to be submitted within five days after receipt of notification in order to expedite consideration of the protest. Unanswered requests for information by the purchasing manager may result in a resolution of the protest without consideration of any information. Upon written request, the purchasing manager makes available to any interested party information submitted that bears on the substance of the protest, except when information is proprietary or otherwise permitted or required to be withheld by law or regulation. A decision on a protest will be made by the purchasing manager in writing after receiving all relevant, requested information. Before issuance, the decision of the purchasing manager should be reviewed by the organization's attorney.

RECOMMENDATION OF AWARD

After all your work and due diligence, you are finally able to make a recommendation to the purchasing department for the firm with the best overall rank. The evaluation team is now finished with its intended task and can be disbanded. Once approved by the governing body, in my case the CSC, and the purchasing department, the purchasing manager will require a copy of the contract to be used and proceed to process all the paperwork required as outlined in the RFP.

In order to find out which firm will be the overall winner, we need to average the points assigned to the short-listed firms and score them appropriately (see figure 3.3).

The following should be included in their bid packet before contract approval:

1. Fee proposal form
2. Non-collusion certification
3. Affirmative action data form
4. Joint venture eligibility
5. Proof of insurance
6. Signed contract by the organization and the design firm
7. Preliminary project schedule

4

Recommendation of Award

CONTRACT APPROVAL

Your organization may have several types of contracts that perform differently based on the type, size, and scope of the project. It could be for IT software, new computer servers, an office building, or another facility. The contract used will be determined based on what was used on previously approved projects, or on any recently updated and approved contract related to the work performed. In my organization, we use different contracts developed in-house or semi-customized. Published boilerplate documents, such as the Engineers Joint Contract Documents Committee (EJCDC) contracts (see appendix E), are good but need to be tailored to fit your needs and most likely cannot be used outside of the construction industry. Because of that, you might only use these documents occasionally.

DOCUMENT DEVELOPMENT

As part of the contract documents, or as an attachment to the contract, you will need to include a scope of services, statement of work (SOW), or steps that the consultant will need to do, based on the work breakdown structure (WBS) dictionary and each WBS component, in order for the firm to be paid. Using the new fire station example in figure 1.1, we can include the following details related to the design portion of the project so that the design firm knows what our expectations are when submitting complete information, before the organization can authorize payment. This list is developed using the milestones/design phases and schedules for payment outlined in the request for proposal (RFP) and the bid form. Basic services and deliverables should include the following items at a minimum and as outlined.[18]

1. Contracted architectural services: As part of basic services that are required to fully design the project in compliance with the terms of the agreement, including drawings that are complete, accurate, and constructible, the design firms agreement for services consists of all work necessary to complete on time each of the deliverables and services described in parts 2 through 6 below. This includes all subconsultant work required per the RFP and the contract, along with any design and engineering services necessary to produce accurate and complete documents that are constructible.
   a. Subconsulting firms for structural, civil, mechanical, electrical, and plumbing design services do not relieve the architect from any errors and/or omissions of the subconsultant and the architect remains responsible for those errors and/or omissions.
   b. The design firm is to perform tasks outlined in the RFP and the contract before and during construction until final as-builts are approved.
2. Schematic and design development phases (15%–35% DD): The design firm duties include the following:
   a. Meet with the organization and confirm the project scope, sometimes referred to as a kick-off meeting.
   b. Visit the site and make recommendations regarding the structures constructability. A geotechnical engineer may be required to test the ground per the contract agreement to provide footing design options and pavement sections.
   c. Outline the local codes that will apply to the project and submit a report to the owner for review.
   d. A charette or design meeting will be needed once the site has been deemed constructible.
   e. A summary of square footage, net and gross, must be prepared and submitted to the organization's representative for review and comment.
   f. The architect needs to attend and prepare required documents for all meetings with code agencies and commissioning boards for project design approvals.
   g. Provide any alternative designs for review.
   h. After review and comments from the organization regarding the 15% schematic design have been addressed through any required iterations, written approval to proceed to the next phase is granted and the design firm can move onto the 35% design development documents (DDs).

This submission should include a draft outline of the project manual and be submitted to the organization for review and comment. The area summary, civil, structural, HVAC, and mechanical, electrical, and plumbing (MEP) systems design calculations shall be part of this submission.

   i. Delivery of a third-party professional cost estimate to the reviewer for review and comment within two weeks from submitting the final schematic design drawings is required. The design firm's detailed documentation supporting the estimate shall be included with the submission. Payment for this work will not be processed until the cost estimate has been received by the organization.

   j. Furnish electronic drawing files of the schematic floor plans in both CADD version 14 or higher and PDF formats for record-keeping.

   k. As parts of the allowance (professional quality renderings), prepare a design model and/or photorealistic three-dimensional rendering of the project's exterior elevations in perspective, including colored site and floor plans. Submit them for review and approval by the organization's representatives.

   l. Review and respond to comments and provide iterations before starting the next phase and include changes in the next design phase.

3. Construction document phase (50% CD): The design firm duties include the following:

   a. Meet with the organization and refine the project plan. A keying meeting will also be required and may be combined in this meeting.

   b. Prepare a furnishings and equipment layout.

   c. Prepare door, hardware, and finish schedules, and color board depicting wall, floor, and ceiling finishes, and submit them to the organization's representative for review and comment.

   d. Develop construction documents (50% CD), and outline project manual specifications. Submit for review and comment to organization's representative all significant calculations related to all civil, structural, HVAC, and MEP systems, along with a cost estimate with recommendations for these systems.

   e. Prepare a statement of estimated costs, attach it to the professional cost estimator's report, and submit it to the organization's representative for review and comment within two weeks following submittal of the 50% CD drawings. Submit in the format mentioned in section 2j above. Provide greater detail. The design firm detailed documentation supporting the estimate needs to be submitted to the organization's representative. The documentation shall include the 50% CD estimate addressing significant changes from the previous estimate. The

50% CD phase cost estimate shall clearly indicate, by line item, major changes between the cost estimates from the 35% DD phase and the 50% CD phase. Payment for this work will not be processed until the cost estimate has been received by the organization's representative having approval authority.

f. Apply for and pay any fees required for permits related to the project. Provide necessary support and attend all meetings with regulatory agencies.

g. Once approved by the owner's representative, incorporate comments into the documents as directed by the owner's representative.

h. Apply for and pay all fees required for permits to obtain a building permit for the project. Provide all support regarding comments or questions the agencies may have and attend all meetings with regulatory agencies. Revise the project documents as needed for approval at no additional cost to the organization.

4. Construction documents phase (95% CD): The design firm duties include the following:

a. Generate a final finish schedule for the project and submit it to the organization's representative for approval. The approved finish schedule shall be incorporated into the project documents and project manual.

b. Prepare 95% construction drawings, specifications, and bid documents setting forth in detail all requirements for the construction of the project, and submit them to the organization's representative for review and comment. The design firm shall be responsible for all project documents related to technical adequacy, professional quality, and the coordination of all designs, drawings, and project manuals, along with any other services furnished under the agreement, and constructability of the project and bid documents. The design firm's construction documents shall depict a project that complies with all ordinances and codes. The design consultant shall submit, with the construction documents, an indexed copy of all design calculations to include structural, HVAC, and MEP systems design. The organization will furnish the design firm copies of the general conditions (front-end documents) of the project manual for the insertion of supplemental general conditions, special conditions, invitation to bid, and instructions to bidders, along with a construction contract(s) for incorporation into the contract documents.

c. Submit to the organization's representative two sealed sets of the approved bid set for final review.

d. Prepare a construction document phase statement of estimated costs, attach it to the professional cost estimator's report, and submit it to the organization's representative for review and comment within two weeks following submittal of the 95% CD drawings. The submitted format shall be consistent with the previous estimate but shall provide greater detail as to all costs. The design firm detailed documentation supporting such estimate shall be submitted to the organization's representative. Submit a narrative with the 95% CD phase submission addressing significant changes from the previous estimate and any assumptions. The 95% CD phase cost estimate shall clearly indicate, by line item, major changes between the cost estimates for the 50% CD phase and the 95% CD phase. Payment for this work will not be processed until the cost estimate has been received by the organization. If substantial design work is required to address the changes, the design firm must inform the owner's representative that substantial additional design work will require additional costs. However, if the estimate is over the established construction budget originally established, the design firm must provide changes to bring the design back into budget at no additional costs.

    e. Revise any interior designs.

    f. Attend and provide all required design changes, comments, and responses at meetings with regulatory agencies having jurisdiction regarding the project.

5. Bidding document phase (100% bid set): The design firm duties include the following:

    a. Based on written comments and directions from the organization's representative, revise the construction documents and project manual and submit copies of complete documents in order to issue/execute a bid.

6. Bid phase: The design firm shall assist with bidding and negotiation activities, as follows:

    a. Participate in pre-bid conferences with the organization's representative and potential contractors, subcontractors, and suppliers.

    b. Consult with the organization and/or the purchasing manager to develop, assemble, and distribute all bid packages to prospective bidders.

    c. The organization will determine the bidding schedule and the design firm will incorporate it into the project manual.

    d. Respond to potential contractor, subcontractor, and supplier requests for information (RFIs), and prepare required addenda that will be published by the purchasing manager.

    e. Bid opening participation is optional but strongly suggested.

    f. Post-bid review, verification of bids, and recommendations will be done by the purchasing manager and the organization's representative, based on bidders being responsive and responsible. The design firm shall be available to provide reviews and recommendations upon request.

   g. Inform the organization's representative if any changes in requirements result in an adjustment in the estimated construction costs.

   h. Furnish the organization's representative with electronic drawing files of the construction documents per the format mentioned in section 2j.

7. Construction administration phase: The design firm duties include the following:

   a. Participate in a preconstruction meeting with the organization's representatives, the contractor, subcontractors, and suppliers for the project. Additionally, attend all construction progress meetings (standard schedule is every two weeks).

   b. Clarify and correct any inaccuracies and errors and/or omissions in the drawings, project manual, or other project documents that are prepared by the design firm or its subconsultants. Review and approve all submittals, shop drawings, and materials. Shop drawings must be submitted in accordance to the project manual. Verify all color matches selected. The design firm shall not be responsible for any submissions different from that of the project documents. The design firm's review and approval, or notes, shall meet the requirements of the general conditions outlined in the project manual. The design firm shall maintain a submittal log for reference during the construction phase of the project.

   c. Prepare bulletins and/or construction change directives (CCDs), at no cost to the organization, due to conflicts regarding interpretation of the project manual and any contract documents related to the conflict that were prepared by the design firm or its subconsultants. The design firm shall provide the organization with an estimate of the cost before notifying the contractor.

   d. Be familiar with the responsibilities of the design firm as outlined in the contract documents and expanded upon in this document. These responsibilities include coordination between the design firm and the contractor.

   e. Send two sets of approved, stamped, and sealed documents/prints per the directions of the organization's representative.

   f. Visit the project site to inspect the progress and quality of the work and determine if the work is per the project documents. Work that is noncompliant is to be rejected in writing by the design firm. The design firm will need to inform the organization's representative and the contractor of any deficiencies, in a report detailing the findings of each deficiency. The design firm shall inform the organization's representative regarding construction progress and any work that can potentially hold up substantial completion and use and occupancy (U&O),

proactively protecting the organization from defects and deficiencies in the work.

g. Participate, as necessary, in meetings that involve code compliance and inspections by code officials, and prepare any documents or provide direction related to the project at no additional cost to the organization.

h. Conduct preliminary, open ceiling, rough-in, and final inspections of the work and develop a punch list for final completion. Re-inspect the work to verify corrections, at no additional cost to the organization.

i. Prepare and submit project drawings within 30 days of the firm obtaining redlined as-built from the contractor. Submit one hard copy and one electronic file of the as-builts, with markups shown red in color. The format should be in a form acceptable to the organization.

j. When the punch list is completed and inspections approved, along with U&O, the design firm must provide written notice to the organization's representative that the work has been completed per the project documents.

k. Receive and review operation and maintenance manuals (O&Ms) and attend any start-up meetings.

l. Review all RFIs, change order requests (CORs), and proposed change orders (PCOs) from the contractor, and write recommendations to the organization's representative regarding costs and other factors.

m. Prepare and submit to the organization's representative a list of items to be delivered as outlined in the project documents, including O&Ms, stocking items, additional parts, and training manuals.

n. Respond to the organization's representative regarding assistance in the start-up of equipment as required.

o. Inspect the project before final payment is issued to the contractor, assuring that all warranties required for the project have been submitted and activated.

p. Revise the project documents in regard to change orders or construction change directives at no additional cost to the organization.

q. The design firm and organization have no control regarding the contractor's means and/or methods of construction.

r. At the request of the organization's representative, the design firm will interpret and decide the intent of the project documents, and will provide written recommendations.

8. Organization's right to disapprove: The organization has the right to disapprove any portion of the design firm's work within reason. The design firm will make a good faith attempt to gain the owner's approval regarding their objections, at no additional cost to the organization.

ALLOWANCES

Allowances are an important part of a project's overall success. They identify work that is needed but established based on a rough cost, with a fee not to exceed amount. This will save time in the overall schedule by eliminating wasteful and time-consuming layers of bureaucracy. For example, with allowances, the design firm will be compensated for work identified in the allowance section of the RFP and the contract. Items that are considered allowances can be for reimbursable expenses, such as mileage, parking fees, and postage. Renderings or geotechnical services can also be assigned an estimated allowance value. If no allowances are identified before a contract is executed, a change order would be required for all these expenses and would eventually slow the project down substantially because of the time it would take to negotiate and process all of the individual change orders. With allowances, design firms would simply include the backup information as part of their invoice, identifying that those costs are associated with an allowance identified during the RFP and in the contract.

In addition to the fee for basic services, the following allowances have been established to provide the work described, when and as directed by the PM. The design firm must include these allowances as part of their base fee proposal. These allowances are established for the purpose of obtaining a consistent fee proposal between bidders. Should the actual cost of the services be less than or greater than the allowance amount, a change order will be issued to adjust the contract amount accordingly. The organization will also have the opportunity to adjust or eliminate any or all of the allowances prior to the award of the design contract.

1. Geotechnical services: This allowance is established to provide compensation for the hiring of a geotechnical consultant to perform a complete and comprehensive subsurface soils investigation for the project, including the preparation and submittal of a final geotechnical report. Compensation for this work will be paid under this allowance for the direct cost of these services times a 1.10 multiplier ($10,000.00).
2. Reimbursable expenses: This allowance is established to provide compensation for reimbursable expenses incurred by the design firm in connection with this project as defined under section 4.16 in the RFP. Compensation for this work will be paid under this allowance for the direct cost to the design firm times a 1.10 multiplier ($10,000.00).
3. Professional-quality renderings (photorealistic three-dimensional rendering): This allowance is established for the purpose of obtaining professional quality renderings to illustrate the design concepts for use in presentations, marketing efforts, and press releases ($5,000.00).

It is important to note that if the designer is getting close to the established upset limit of the allowance, they need to inform the PM, or vice-versa, and any additional costs assigned to that allowance will produce a deficit. In this case, we would simply develop a change order including the deficit amount and an educated guess for funds that are not yet realized. For example, using the above-mentioned rendering allowance amount of $5,000.00, your designer informs you that the renderings will cost $4,500.00, leaving a balance of $500.00. After this work is completed and submitted, the organization decides that it would like an additional rendering showing a different perspective. The designer informs you that the additional work will cost $3,000.00. In order for the designer to proceed with the additional work, the project manager needs to execute a user-requested change order in the amount of $2,500.00. In addition to this amount, and in case the users need additional renderings, or have another request that is related to rendering, additional money will be needed. At this point, you would want to include in the change order an additional, let's say, $3,000.00 for services to pay for unknown conditions. So the total change order amount would be $5,500.00. The $3,000.00 would be considered a contingency amount, which is what we will discuss next.

CONTINGENT ITEMS

Unlike allowances, contingent items are used as a predetermined amount of money to be used for unpredictable changes in a project. Contingencies can pay for design changes, price escalation, necessary construction design changes, and errors and/or omissions. Depending on your organization's policies regarding contingencies, it may be standard operating procedure (SOP) to use a contingency amount for design contracts of 10% of the original fee amount. Say a firm provides a fee proposal in the amount of $180,000.00; not including allowances, you would need to add a contingency amount of $18,000.00 to the overall recommendation for award.

Since a contingency amount can be considered extra or special services, the rules identifying what is compensable and noncompensable need to be outlined in the RFP.

REIMBURSABLE EXPENSES

A reimbursable expense is an allowance that pays for any expenses above those included in the design firm's basic services. Reimbursable expenses should be outlined and identified in the RFP and again in the contract so that no misunderstanding takes place between the design firm and the organization. In the RFP, qualifying reimbursable expenses are described in detail and can include printing, reproduction, plots, and photography. The tricky part about reimbursable expenses is that any printing, reproduction, plots, and photography used to provide information between the design firm and their sub-consultants are not considered reimbursable expenses and should be included in their basic services, not in the reimbursable expenses allowance. If plots, printing, reproductions, and photography are produced for the organization's use, then these can be invoiced against the reimbursable allowance. Making sure the right allowance is billed correctly can save you time when processing invoices. So be sure to examine any sections of any contracts that call for including reimbursable expenses, so that no double-billing occurs.

5

Executing the Design Phase

STANDARD OPERATING PROCEDURES (SOPS)

Having a similar result as an owner's project requirements (OPR) and building standards checklist, standard operating procedures (SOPs) are written instructions detailing all steps and activities of a process or procedure. Documentation of all procedures is required to achieve an organization's means and methods regarding how it wants procedures followed and tasks executed. For example, you may need instructions on how to set up a keying meeting. If your organization has an SOP log, you would simply look up the procedure and follow the directions. If none exists, you would develop the SOP for approval and publication.

BUILDING STANDARDS

In order for your project to conform to the operational side of the finished project, your organization may have a building standards checklist (see appendix B) so that maintenance and facilities services departments can maintain the building after completing the project. The organization could have standards that go above and beyond what is considered industry standards. By setting up a building standard meeting with maintenance and faculties services you can develop a building standards checklist, unless one already exists. For example, the maintenance department may only use white paint from one manufacturer, or may require using only one hardware manufacturer for door hardware. The sample RFP in appendix B outlines an example of what may be required by maintenance.

OWNER'S PROJECT REQUIREMENTS (OPR)

When a maintenance department needs to make sure heating and cooling systems operate per their desired requirements, they meet with the PM to develop a priority list of requirements. This is referred to as an OPR.[19] It is typically included in the RFP (see appendix B). For instance, maintenance may have five priorities when the design firm develops the heating, ventilation, and air conditionings (HVAC) systems. They may want the following items considered during design, with the first item being a priority. This will allow the design firm to design a system that may cost more to operate over the life cycle of the building, but will provide more comfort. An example might be to provide thermostats in every room in the building.

1. Comfort and system reliability
2. Temperature and humidity control
3. Energy management practices
4. System energy efficiency
5. Life cycle costs

As part of the OPR, our organization may request commissioning services provided by a third-party firm that specializes in building systems commissioning. They might be listed as a subconsultant in the RFP, and a detailed outline of services required would be listed there. Because we typically do not request this service, I have listed some of the services that your organization may want if obtaining commissioning services:

1. The owner shall provide the commissioning firm the OPR outlined in the RFP.
2. The commissioning firm's duties entail the following:
   a. Develop a commissioning plan based on the approved OPR.
   b. Develop a daily log of issues to track and document any deviations relating to the owner's project requirements.
   c. Prepare progress reports for meetings.
3. Design commissioning activities pre-design:
   a. Verify commissioning service activities.
   b. Develop a cost and schedule of commissioning service activities.
   c. Track and modify any deviations/recommendation related to the approved OPR.
   d. Review design documents at each phase of design to ensure the OPR is being integrated into the project as planned.

   e. Update the commissioning plan.

   f. Write a commissioning progress report.

4. Design commission activities for design documents to bid set:

   a. Provide review and recommendations of systems and assembly options.

   b. Review calculations and sizing of ductwork.

   c. Review system makes and models.

   d. Review operational aspects of the equipment.

   e. Coordinate findings with design firm.

   f. Provide a report describing any requirements that cannot be implemented and why, along with recommended alternatives.

5. Design commissioning activities for construction:

   a. Develop a checklist for equipment, pre-installation meetings, installation checks.

   b. Review and approve system submittals.

   c. Review and approve maintenance manuals for use and operation.

   d. Develop equipment testing procedures.

   e. Execute testing procedures with maintenance.

   f. Verify that maintenance has been trained properly for safe operation of equipment.

6. Design commissioning activities after U&O and during operation:

   a. Provide ongoing support and training for a year after U&O.

   b. Provide call-back support to the contractor for system deficiencies.

   c. Provide a final project commissioning report.

Before adding the OPR to the RFP, it is important to get the organization's maintenance representatives to sign off on the list of priorities so that the agreement can be recorded into the project record.

PROGRAM

Once an organization has identified a need for space, they may require services to develop a program. This can be done by executing a task order under a previously approved IDQ (see appendix C) for architectural services. The PM would develop a request for quote (RFQ) describing the services required. It could be a preliminary space study to develop a floor plan, along with a site feasibility study to see if the building will fit on the proposed purchase or on already owned land. Detailed services requested could include the size and description of rooms based on the organization's space standards and requirements, functionality of the space, design requirements and expectations, identifying any existing structures, providing environmental studies, geotechnical service to develop proposed foundation and pavement designs, renovation requirements, demolition requirements, ancillary spaces, site plan requirements, environmental site design requirements, stormwater management requirements, future expansion requirements, special equipment, proposed budget for construction, and so on.

In some cases you may already have an approved program based on a previous but similar project. This would help save the organization some money by utilizing the existing study and eliminating the program stage of design.

KICK-OFF MEETING

This is the first meeting held by the project manager, who is the gatekeeper for this task, before the firm is given a notice to proceed (NTP), which is the official start date of the contracted work. The project manager develops an agenda for the meeting and will take notes for meeting minutes. Starting the meeting off with introductions between the key personnel and the design team is essential. Passing around a sign-in sheet and a copy of the agenda before starting introductions will help you keep better records when generating meeting minutes.

Invitations are sent to the following users/stakeholders:

- User agency contact
- Maintenance personnel
- Management services personnel
- IIT personnel
- Design firm and their subconsultants

An agenda should include items that will clearly identify the project's starting point when all the people involved can go over future milestones. Some basic items included in the agenda are as listed below:

- List of attendees
- Verify users, stakeholders, and design teams
- Discuss the scope of the project
- Review the budget
- Discuss preliminary schedule for design; go over the design phases and what the design team must provide at each phase
- Set notice to proceed date for design

- Develop and identify any required permits and potential fees
- Brainstorm potential issues
- Identify equipment such as furnishings, both movable and permanent
- Discuss any items that require hazardous abatement
- Provide the design team with any standards that need incorporated in the design, such as specific equipment and standards required by maintenance as part of the economy of scale philosophy

The list of attendees will need to include each person's name, company or office, e-mail address, and phone numbers (work and fax). Verifying users is a simple but necessary task to identify your architect, engineers, and their disciplines; it also gives everyone a chance to understand each other's role in the project.

The project scope and budget review will list specific details related to the project so that everyone is in agreement that this is what we have asked the contracted firm to provide.

Go over the design phases and the preliminary schedule for design, explaining submission due dates, length of review time for users at each submission, when cost estimates are required, and the process of submitting comments to the project manager. Comments generated by users are combined into one document that is forwarded to the design team so that the team can make changes to the documents for the next submission.

Notice to proceed may have been set once the contract is signed. In most cases NTP is set at the kick-off meeting with all in attendance agreeing on establishing the start date, submittal due dates, permit submission dates, schedule of values, and a preliminary construction timeline indicating when the project will be substantially complete and ready for use and occupancy.

SCHEMATIC DESIGN

After the program has been established and findings of the feasibility study have determined that the existing program will fit the proposed site, the design firm provides an initial design that will eventually meet all the requirements of zoning and site plan approval by a planning commission or other approval agency. The amount of time typically allotted for this task is 30 calendar days from start to submission.

In your request for services you may need to ask that the design firm provide several different options regarding floor plans. Several iterations by the design firm may be required before the organization signs off on the schematic, allowing the design firm to move on to the next stage of design. If required, the estimate must also be submitted for review by the PM to make sure the project is within the established budget provided by the organization. If not, the design firm will need to revise and resubmit the documents so that the project complies with the budget. The PM is the gatekeeper for this process. They distribute documents to the organization's users, allowing them time, about 21 calendar days, to review and comment. During the 21-day review period the organization may also want a peer review performed as part of the review process. The PM will need to be sure that the drawings include what the organization may require. Using project management philosophies, this task would be considered a review based on quality control measures. The following design phases, schematic design through 95% CDs, are a checklist of items to review before approving design submissions.[20]

It is important to note that summations of deliverables for DD and CD phases are to be preceded by a complete point-by-point response to the comments generated on the previous phase of design work. Also, as a general rule, submissions should not have an individual volume of drawings exceeding 25 pounds in weight, and no individual specification book volume should exceed 3 inches in thickness.

- ☐ Scope of work narrative
- ☐ List of applicable codes on the drawing title sheet
- ☐ Building code review
- ☐ List of anticipated building code variance requests
- ☐ Anticipated building and space occupancy schedules
- ☐ Life safety (egress) plans identifying security and access control points
- ☐ Owner's project requirements as described in the RFP
- ☐ System and material narrative description
- ☐ Review preliminary schedule of building materials to be used

- ☐ Preliminary project manual outline developed and submitted
- ☐ Cost estimate review, if required by the organization at this stage. The estimate must be within the established budget
- ☐ If obtaining LEED (leadership in energy and environmental design) certification and/or commissioning services, make sure a sustainability work session is held and review the schematic documents to see if LEED practices have been incorporated

Once an organization's comments have been answered with point-by-point responses in writing, and/or iterations have been submitted by the design firm and approved by the PM per the organization's combined responses, and the project has remained within the originally established budget, the PM can then give the design firm permission to proceed to the next design phase, the 35% design development (35% DD) phase, and apply for preliminary site plan review to the local jurisdiction having authority. Your local planning department, zoning office, or development review office (engineering and planning) should be able to help point you in the proper direction if you have questions.

35% DESIGN DEVELOPMENT DOCUMENTS (35% DD)

While developing the 35% design development documents, the design firm is typically allotted 30 calendar days from start date to submission due date.

In the schematic design you should have approved the foundation plan and the general footprint of the building; this allows the design firm to start providing greater detail, knowing that parameters for the foundation or exterior walls have been established, and to work within those parameters.

The PM is the gatekeeper for this process, and it distributes documents to the organization's users for review and comment. The time allotted depends on the experience the organization's users have with reviewing development documents, so a typical time allotment may be as little as 14 calendar days up to 21 calendar days. Several iterations by the design firm may be required before the organization signs off on the 35% DDs, allowing the design firm to move on to the next stage of design. If required, the estimate, which will have greater detail than the previous estimate, must also be submitted for review by the PM to make sure the project is within established budgets provided by the organization. If not, the design firm will need to revise and resubmit the documents so that the project complies with the budget at no additional cost to the organization.

The following is a checklist of items to review before approving the submittal:

☐ Existing conditions
☐ Building outline
☐ Future expansion
☐ Site entrance
☐ Roads and driveways
☐ Parking locations
☐ Loading space
☐ Waste/recycling collection/ storage locations
☐ Walkway locations

☐ Utility requirements: gas, water, sewer, telecom, TV, storm drains, electric, oil separator, and vent piping detail
☐ Site utilities
☐ Preliminary grading plan
☐ Soil erosion and sedimentation control plan
☐ Preliminary site lighting plan

- ☐ Photometric plan with calculations
- ☐ Exterior signage
- ☐ Life safety/fire signage requirements
- ☐ Pre-emption device locations
- ☐ Road signage
- ☐ Proposed locations of vehicle and pedestrian traffic controls
- ☐ Accessible parking (handicapped spaces)
- ☐ Grading plan (cut/fill calculations)
- ☐ Utility plans showing profiles/ elevations, pipe sizes and types, invert elevations and details
- ☐ Sewer flow calculations
- ☐ Dewatering plan (if needed)
- ☐ Apply for final site plan approval through planning/ zoning office
- ☐ Topographical plan indicating two vertical and horizontal control points
- ☐ Generator size and location
- ☐ Landscaping plan and details
- ☐ Guying diagrams
- ☐ Landscape and irrigation details
- ☐ 10-year color photo of growth plan
- ☐ Color-contrasted landscape plan
- ☐ Structural scheme plans
- ☐ Written description
- ☐ Typical elevations
- ☐ Fenestration plan
- ☐ Overall building sections: north, south, east, west
- ☐ Roof layout
- ☐ Typical floor plans (min. 1/8" scale) with legends

- ☐ Dimension floor plans
- ☐ Floor plans for room and door numbering
- ☐ Area use identification & area in square feet
- ☐ Mechanical, electrical, IIT, janitor, and other service closets/rooms
- ☐ Circulations paths
- ☐ Area tabulations compared to program requirements
- ☐ Show flexibility for expansion and alterations
- ☐ Preliminary layout of major spaces with fixed equipment
- ☐ Identify all systems and incorporate OPR into HVAC design
- ☐ One-line diagrams for each air, hydronic, stem, condensate and all other HVAC-related systems, and other materials as required to describe the fundamental design concept for all mechanical systems
- ☐ Induction of the amount of redundancy for all major pieces of mechanical equipment (if needed)
- ☐ Major equipment locations
- ☐ Air intake and discharge locations
- ☐ Color-coded gross HVAC zoning plan, and typical individual space zoning (i.e., VAV boxes per office)
- ☐ Mechanical legend
- ☐ Special occupancy zones
- ☐ One-line (riser) diagrams for every plumbing system

(domestic water, sanitary, storm, gas, etc.) and other materials as required describing the fundamental design concept for all plumbing systems
- ☐ Indication of the amount of redundancy for all major pieces of mechanical equipment
- ☐ Main water supply, storm, and sanitary leads
- ☐ Locker and restroom locations
- ☐ Plumbing legend
- ☐ Foundation, slab, and floor drains
- ☐ One-line diagrams for each fire protection system and other materials as required describing the fundamental design concept for all fire protection systems
- ☐ Report documenting adequacy of utility
- ☐ Connection to utility
- ☐ Location of fire pump and controller, jockey pump, and sprinkler valves
- ☐ Sprinkler legend
- ☐ Electrical symbols legend
- ☐ General drawing notes
- ☐ General photometric levels
- ☐ Fixture, lamp, and controls descriptions
- ☐ Preliminary outdoor lighting plans
- ☐ Preliminary emergency generator package (size)
- ☐ One-line diagrams with equipment ratings
- ☐ Exterior equipment locations
- ☐ Generator package and ATS descriptions

- ☐ Substation, generator and electric room locations
- ☐ Preliminary generator plans
- ☐ Panel numbering scheme
- ☐ System description
- ☐ FA panel locations
- ☐ Preliminary FA device and appliance location plans (ceiling mounted strobes only)
- ☐ Manhole, duct bank, and building entry locations
- ☐ Building entrance and local telephone room/IIT locations
- ☐ Riser diagram
- ☐ Preliminary cable tray plans
- ☐ Access control meeting
- ☐ Special materials and systems
- ☐ Professional rendering (photorealistic 3D)
- ☐ Movable furnishings and artwork locations (furnishings and artwork details are to be provided by the organization)
- ☐ If obtaining a LEED certification and requiring commissioning services, make sure a sustainability work session is held and review the schematic documents to see if LEED practices have been incorporated.
- ☐ Review schedule of building materials to be used
- ☐ Specifications outline developed and submitted
- ☐ Cost estimate review, if required by the organization at this stage. Estimate must be within the established budget

KEYING MEETING

The purpose of a keying meeting is to identify the roles and responsibilities of the PM with regard to door hardware and keying. This will allow coordination between the building users and maintenance staff to identify keying needs that will be incorporated in renovation and/or new construction projects. The PM will initiate this discussion with maintenance, locksmith, management services, and the intended facility users to obtain a better understanding of their plans for facility use. This information should be incorporated in the facility design to support the user's operational processes.

50% CONSTRUCTION DOCUMENTS (CDS)

The 50% construction document stage starts once approval is granted by the organization to proceed from 35% DDs to 50% CDs. Thirty calendar days should be allotted to the design firm for this task. Included in the 50% CDs should be the review tasks mentioned in the 35% DDs, with greater detail provided. The following is a checklist of items to review before approving the submittal.

- ☐ Planting plan finalized
- ☐ Irrigation plan or watering plan with estimated water usage per year
- ☐ Foundation plan and details including rebar ledged and details
- ☐ Typical framing plans
- ☐ Framing details of unique features
- ☐ Member sizing plan
- ☐ Structural sections
- ☐ Structural details
- ☐ Structural notes
- ☐ Structural calculations
- ☐ Structural wall details, including rebar details if needed
- ☐ All building elevations w/ dimensional heights
- ☐ Typical wall sections
- ☐ Parapet, coping, and cricket details
- ☐ Roof and drainage plan
- ☐ Exterior door details
- ☐ Typical window details
- ☐ Expansion joint locations
- ☐ Any required large-scale cross-sections
- ☐ All floor plans (min. 1/8" scale)
- ☐ Enlarged plans at elevation changes (i.e., steps if used)
- ☐ Enlarged plans at locker and toilet rooms
- ☐ Reflected ceiling plans
- ☐ Wall types, fire ratings, smoke control zones
- ☐ Keying meeting hardware details
- ☐ Occupancy capacity
- ☐ Signage details

- ☐ Flammable liquids storage cabinet location
- ☐ Fixed seating
- ☐ Details of unique features of the site and building details of fixed equipment
- ☐ Preliminary finish schedule
- ☐ Preliminary door schedule
- ☐ Overall building air flow diagram indicating air handlers, exhaust fans, duct risers, and duct mains, including any calculations
- ☐ Duct access door locations
- ☐ Plans indicating shaft, mechanical chase, and recess requirements
- ☐ Equipment locations with enlarged mechanical plans
- ☐ Indication of typical locations of fire dampers, smoke dampers, and combination f/s dampers
- ☐ Control diagrams (concept form) for all mechanical and plumbing systems
- ☐ Outline of major control sequences of operation
- ☐ Mechanical/electrical smoke control schemes
- ☐ Preliminary floor plans of mechanical rooms with all components and required service access areas drawn to scale
- ☐ Preliminary calculations
- ☐ Meter locations and types
- ☐ Updated design criteria for each plumbing system (including set points, water quality levels, etc.)
- ☐ Preliminary piping plans for all systems

- ☐ Backflow prevention (BFP) locations (include on 2" truck fills mounted on engine bay wall)
- ☐ Fixture schedules
- ☐ Equipment schedules
- ☐ Water riser diagram, including assumed fixture counts per floor connection
- ☐ Waste and vent riser diagrams including assumed fixture counts per floor connection
- ☐ Foundation, slab, and floor drains finalized
- ☐ Location of test headers and fire department connection (FDC)
- ☐ Preliminary piping plans
- ☐ Fire pump sizing calculations
- ☐ Fire station alert system riser
- ☐ Fire station alert system integration details (into watch room equipment)
- ☐ Thrust block detail (if required)
- ☐ Preliminary interior lighting plans
- ☐ Typical interior lighting and control plans
- ☐ Outdoor lighting and control plans
- ☐ Fixture types and schedule
- ☐ Control system and control device descriptions
- ☐ Typical photometric calculations
- ☐ Dimming, daylighting and low voltage control zones
- ☐ Manhole, duct bank, and building entry plans and details
- ☐ Normal power riser diagram with circuit breaker, fuse, conduit and wire sizes

☐ Emergency power riser diagram with circuit breaker, fuse, conduit, and wire sizes
☐ Grounding riser diagram
☐ Fault current and coordination studies used to specify equipment ratings
☐ Substation standard details
☐ List of equipment on emergency power
☐ Electrical load calculations
☐ Panel schedules
☐ Typical panel arc flash and color code labels
☐ Electrical equipment locations plans
☐ Typical electrical outlet location plans (power plans)
☐ Plan for temporary power during construction
☐ FA riser diagram
☐ FA panel, device, and appliance location plans

☐ Conduit and cable tray plans with conduit and cable tray sizes
☐ Follow maintenance standards checklist and OPRs
☐ Typical voice, data outlet locations plan
☐ Access control locations
☐ Review any special materials and systems
☐ Site plans need to show stabilized construction entrance, limits of disturbance (LOD), building restriction lines, topsoil stockpile location
☐ The project manual should be 95% completed
☐ If obtaining a LEED certification and requiring commissioning services, make sure a sustainability work session is held and review the schematic documents to see if LEED practices have been incorporated

As part of this submission, the organization may require another cost estimate. The design firm will also be addressing any permit review comments related to the improvement plans, which will need to be approved before submission for a building permit.

95% CD

The 95% CD stage is started once the organization provides approval of the 50% CDs. The allotted time for this task should be 50 calendar days, with a review time frame of 21 calendar days. At this point in the design PM tasks are similar to those for 50% CDs but the design firm must apply for the building permits. A typical length of time for this review and approval task is 75 days. The project manual should be 98% completed with the front end documents to be added. The PM, purchasing manager, and design firm will coordinate the front end documents for publishing. Most purchasing departments and project management offices will have a boilerplate of front end documents that can be tailored to fit your specific project (see appendix D). Once approved by the organization, a constructability review can take place concurrent with or while generating the final 100% bid set. The following is a checklist of items to review before approving the submittal.

- Extent of construction area
- Area traffic plan (roads/walks impacted)
- Site development phasing
- Construction site access
- Apply for grading permit application
- Identification (ID) staging area
- Construction signage
- Site details (including hardscape)
- Finalized utility profiles
- Connection details
- Approved building permits and grading permit
- Planting specifications
- Protection for any existing trees and plantings to remain during construction
- Soil preparations and planting specifications
- Landscape details
- Control joint locations and details
- Beam, column, and slab schedules
- Mechanical and electrical concrete housekeeping pads
- Foundation details finalized
- Structural details finalized
- Structural notes finalized
- Finalized structural calculations
- Roof-mounted equipment
- Roof details
- Exterior details
- Flashing details
- Control joint definitions and details
- Dimensioned floor plans finalized
- Enlarged plans finalized
- Partition details
- Interior details
- Interior elevations
- Exterior elevations
- Color scheme development with user agency
- Finish schedules
- Door and hardware schedules
- Evacuation plan details
- Interior signage for rooms and doors
- Schedule of proposed movable equipment that is not indicated on the documents (for reference)
- Detailed piping and duct design with all sizes indicated
- Floor plans with all components and required service access areas. Plans need to indicate duct sizes and air flow quantities relative to each room, including CFM in and out of all doors
- Indicate location of control panels
- Detailed floor plans of mechanical rooms with all components and required service access areas drawn to scale

☐ Cross-sections through mechanical rooms and areas where there are installations/ coordination issues (i.e., tight spaces, zoning of utilities)

☐ In common mechanical space, indication of space zoning by system

☐ Connection to fire alarm and campus control systems, including web based control at another location

☐ Equipment details, including structural support requirements

☐ Installation details

☐ Duct construction schedule (on the drawings), indicating materials and pressure class for each duct system

☐ Detailed controls drawings, including clear differentiation of trade responsibility for control, fire, and control power wiring

☐ Detailed sequences of operations including the specific setpoints for all control loops that will result in attainment of the required design criteria, as well as alarm setpoints and time delays

☐ Water riser diagram, including assumed fixture counts

☐ Detailed piping design with all pipe sizes indicated

☐ Typical plumbing details, including structural support requirements

☐ Water heating piping details

☐ Design calculations

☐ Fire protection service entrance details

☐ Fire protection plans (include header and riser layout) with indication of any required service access areas

☐ Location of all sprinkler zone valves, drains, and fire hose connections

☐ Zoning extents, for areas where the contractor will size the piping

☐ Typical sprinkler installation details, including structural support details

☐ Penetration/sleeve details

☐ Fire alarm system riser

☐ Emergency alert system lighting control

☐ Interior and exterior lighting plans, including control systems and devices, lighting panels, switching and circuiting

☐ Lighting control system schematics and wiring diagrams

☐ Lighting control system detailed sequences of operations

☐ Installation details, including structural support details

☐ Normal lighting photometric calculations

☐ Emergency lighting photometric calculations on 2' grid (if needed)

☐ General notes on conduit and wire sizes for lighting branch circuits

☐ Details of power service to building

☐ Power plans, including primary cable raceways, feeder conduits, electrical loads, duplex and

special receptacles, and circuiting
- ☐ Emergency power system plans, controls, and details
- ☐ Connections to other building systems, including fire alarm, HVAC systems, emergency alert system
- ☐ Details of nonstandard electrical installations
- ☐ Conduit and wire sizes for services, feeders, and special branch circuits
- ☐ General notes on conduit and wire sizes
- ☐ Notes identifying locations of separate and shared neutrals
- ☐ MCC elevations
- ☐ Grounding details
- ☐ Roof and floor penetration details
- ☐ Settings for contactor-furnished electrical equipment
- ☐ Detailed FA panel, device and appliance location plans

including duct detectors, fire/ smoke dampers, sprinkler flow and tamper switches, monitor and control modules, door hold-opens, door lock releases, etc.
- ☐ Strobe light candela ratings
- ☐ Details of connections to HVAC, fire pump, fire suppression, door hold-open, door lock
- ☐ Detailed sequences of operation
- ☐ Follow maintenance standard's checklist
- ☐ Details of voice, data boxes, and conduits w/ pull strings
- ☐ Details of telecom service to the building
- ☐ Details of emergency alert system and how it ties in with telecom
- ☐ Access control riser
- ☐ Access control notes to provide a box, conduit, and pull string
- ☐ Review special materials and systems

CONSTRUCTABILITY REVIEWS

In an effort to keep your project within the triple constraints discussed in chapter 1, constructability reviews are requested by a PM for evaluation by the department of construction management and inspection (DCMI), or conducted in-house by the PM if the organization does not have a DCMI, or contracted to a construction management company that offers constructability review services. The objective is to identify and minimize risk, reduce costly change orders, maximize construction resources, improve quality, avoid conflicts and disputes, provide more accurate schedules, increase productivity, improve the sequence of construction, enhance quality, improve safety during construction, and also minimize maintenance costs. The maintenance department and/or construction management department should be utilized to perform this review, since they are the subject matter experts. Over time, a

PM will have a better understanding of what items pose more risk than others and will be able to provide some risk avoidance.

The following outline is an example of items to look for when performing a constructability review.[21] Additionally, the materials provided herein represent basic themes and suggested minimums when reviewing design documents for construction.

1. PROJECT MANUAL
   a. Is the strategy for submittal processing, quality control, testing, inspections, pre-installation meetings, and mock-ups suitable and adapted to the project?
   b. Standards:
      • Are appropriate standards of performance, quality, and testing cited?
      • Do they correspond to what is specified and drawn?
      • Are they current? Examples: UL standards, FM standards, ASTM standards
   c. Products: Do all of the specified products match what is drawn or specified? Examples: catalog numbers, model numbers and processes
   d. New Systems, assemblies, products unfamiliar to the local market or designer:
      • Has there been an adequate evaluation?
      • Will unwanted delays result?
      • Are the submittal requirements reasonable?
      • Has the owner been advised of these issues?
   e. Are the specifications formatted according to accepted standards of practice, such as CSI's Manual of Practice, MasterFormat, SectionFormat and PageFormat? (Nonstandard specification formats are not recommended).
   f. Are the warranty strategies coordinated, clear and reasonable? When exposed to the intended uses and environments, such as traffic, solar radiation, thermal cycles and moisture, will the completed construction achieve the life expected by the owner?
   g. Are pre-installation meetings and/or mock-ups required?
   h. Is there boilerplate content that has not been tailored to the subject project?
   i. Sole source and/or proprietary specification:
      • Are there sole source and/or proprietary specification sections?
      • Are they necessary?
      • Will substitutes to proprietary specifications be accepted?

    j. Has the relevant knowledge gained from problems recently experienced on previous projects been carried forward to the subject project?

    k. Additional issues should be added to address any specific issues not included above (reviewer's notes should be part of the review).

2. DRAWINGS

    a. General:

- Are all of the views needed to construct provided, such as plans, elevations, sections, schedules, riser diagrams, and details?
- Are all the necessary supplementary documents provided to define the relevant existing conditions, for example, land surveys, geotechnical, environmental?
- Do all large scale plan views match the smaller scaled views?
- Is the layout and content of each sheet clear, concise, and make sense?
- Is there adequate cross-referencing?
- Have matchlines been used only when absolutely necessary?
- Is all built-in equipment scheduled? Are all of the necessary roughins indicated?
- Are all relevant plane transitions detailed?
- Have the subconsultant disciplines been combed for issues that are unsightly, for example, exposed work that should be concealed by an architectural finish?

    b. Title blocks, scales, symbols, abbreviations, sheet #:

- Are all symbols and abbreviations provided in the appropriate legends?
- Are all scales correctly shown?
- Are the title blocks complete and current?
- Is the drawing-layering, sequencing, and numbering in conformance with CSI's Uniform Drawing System (UDS)?
- Have all of the drawn by and checked by blocks been initialed?
- Have the drawings that are initialed been carefully checked?

    c. Geometry (dimensions, angles, radii, fixed positions, benchmarks, etc.):

- Have all of the dimensions, angles, radii, and fixed benchmarks been established?
- Are there a minimum of two vertical and horizontal control points shown on the drawings?
- Does the above geometric information translate to all of the subconsultant's sheets, where relevant?
- Will all of the construction systems and assemblies fit within the available spaces leaving all of the necessary clearances and tolerances for operational, maintenance, and replacement access?

- Are the site grade elevations, finish floor elevations, and building location footprints coordinated with the other disciplines?
- Are the dimensional strings as simple and clear as possible? Do they all close or can they be easily parity-checked against overall dimensions?
- Are the start points and end points of every dimension unmistakably clear? (Dimensions requiring a construction worker to add or subtract because a dimensional string commences from an unreachable point are derivative dimensions.)
- Have derivation dimensions been avoided or minimized?
- Have all drawings that show a graphic scale been drawn at that scale?
- Will alternate or approved substitutes also fit when the details provided have been developed around a specific manufacturer?

d. Civil:
- Are all relevant controlling datum/benchmarks, property lines, setbacks, easements, rights of way, legal encumbrances, relevant existing conditions, existing and proposed contours, existing and proposed inverts, and limits of construction been indicated?
- Has the electrical engineer's electrical site plan been coordinated with the civil engineering site plans, landscape plans and profiles?
- Are all of the primary utilities shown, connected and coordinated on the MEP documents?
- Do all pipes and structures appear reasonably sized?
- Are all profiles coordinated with the plan views?
- Are all relevant utilities shown on profile sheets where they run close or cross each other?
- Do all exposed surfaces have positive drainage to move water away from potential incursion zones and toward catchments or drain locations?

e. Structural: Are all the relevant primary structural elements shown, sized, scheduled, detailed and coordinated to the extent necessary to construct, for example:
- Substructure:
  - Underpinning?
  - Sheeting and shoring?
  - Footings, piers?
  - Below grade walls?
  - On grade?
  - Raft slabs?
  - Slabs on grade, slab thickenings, grade beams, depressed slabs, troughs, pads?

- Superstructure:
  - Columns?
  - Girders?
  - Beams?
  - Decks?
- Secondary structural elements:
  - Bearing plates?
  - Lintels?
  - Bracing?
  - Bridging?
  - Joints?
  - Clips, connections, etc.?
- Surface treatments:
  - Fireproofing?
  - Waterproofing, coatings, sealers?
- Do all of the structural perimeter overhangs match the architectural, for example, roof overhangs and projections?
- Are all primary utility assemblies coordinated with all below-grade structural foundation and wall conditions?
- Have all of the relevant equipment loads and supports been structurally accommodated and detailed?
- Will the expansion and control joint designs and locations handle the differential movements? Are they coordinated with all the other effected disciplines?
- Shaft and chase penetrations through floors can affect many other design disciplines. Are all penetrations coordinated with all the other effected disciplines?
- Are all structural elements such as footings and columns correctly designated and scheduled?

f. Architectural:
  - General: Do the interior and exterior functions, massing, special organizations, circulation, future expansions, appearance, and quality levels address the programmatic requirements?
  - Exterior enclosure:
    - Primary enclosure systems and assemblies identified and coordinated? Examples: masonry, precast concrete, EIFS, glass and glazing
    - Secondary enclosure elements identified and coordinated? Examples: precast concrete trim, lintels, spandrel beams, knee braces, etc.
  - Exterior enclosure moisture control systems and assemblies identified and coordinated?

- Above-grade examples: roofing, waterproofing, damp proofing, condensation controls, architectural sheet metals and flashings, weeps, caulking, glazing, drainage to daylight
- Below-grade examples: drainage board or gravel, foundation drains, sump pits, french drains
- Exterior enclosure thermal control systems and assemblies: Identified and coordinated? Examples: insulation, caulking, and glazing
- Exterior enclosure connections and details:
  - Interior ceiling and wall locations coordinated with window wall framing?
  - Sill and head flashing?
  - Coatings, priming, galvanizing?
  - Joining of dissimilar materials?
  - Finish hardware?
  - Weld certification requirements?
  - Tolerances and clearances?
  - Expansion design?
  - Maintenance details: for example, strategy for keeping clear critical weeps, gutters?
- Shafts and chases: Will the shafts and chases accommodate all the intended assemblies?
- Finishes:
  - Scope, limits (horizontal and vertical), bulkheads, transitions, and room numbers indicated and coordinated on the finish schedules, reflected ceiling plans, interior and exterior elevations?
  - Are all finishes, special coatings, surface treatments and colors identified and scheduled?
- Casework, built-in equipment, and specialties?
  - Is the scope fully indicated?
  - Will it fit as drawn?
  - Is all of the necessary information provided, for example, the interior/exterior surfaces, hardware, details, specifications, and schedules?
- Doors, frames, and hardware (HW):
  - Is all of the finish HW indicated, specified and coordinated?
  - Are doors, frames and HW assemblies coordinated with required undercuts [to permit air flow], electrified hardware, door security requirements and code requirements?
- Coordinated imbeds, anchors, supports, blocking:
  - Are all concrete imbedded items fully identified and specified?
  - Are all the necessary connection details, anchors, hardware, supports, backing and blocking coordinated, detailed and specified?

g. Conveyance:
  - Are all the necessary dimensional and rough-in requirements indicated and coordinated?
  - Is there a disconnect required at the elevator machine room?
  - Is there a shunt trip required at the elevator shaft?
  - Are the pit requirements fully detailed, for example, rough-in requirements, waterproofing, drains, sump pumps, lights?
  - Is the door circuitry coordinated with the life safety systems?
  - Are the cab details sufficient to price or has a suitable allowance been established?
h. Mechanical:
  - Mechanical, general:
    - Is the design a complete system, from supply connection to termination?
    - Are all sizes provided?
    - Do all sizes appear reasonable?
    - Do they match all the riser diagrams provided?
    - Does each component fit with everything else occupying the same volume?
    - Have the necessary thicknesses of insulation, jackets and housings been considered?
    - Have repeating problems of the past been debugged such as coordination of the starters, disconnects, interlock wiring, smoke detectors, color-coding, stenciling responsibilities?
    - Do all mechanical and architectural reflected ceiling plans match? For example, are the registers, grills and equipment located in the same place mechanically and architecturally?
    - Are all sleeve locations coordinated with concrete?
    - Are required composite coordination drawings specified? Has the composite coordination drawing been specified?
  - HVAC:
    - Are the quantities and sizes provided on all equipment, fixtures, piping, ductwork, controls, special accessories, etc.?
    - Are duct outside sizes including insulation also indicated to ensure the insulation will fit?
    - Are all the required fire dampers indicated in the correct locations?
    - If there are any large duct runs over bathrooms with ceiling mounted toilet partitions, have these conflicts been coordinated?
    - Are the control sequences, such as those pertaining to the kitchen exhaust fans, been coordinated with the fire alarm system and the local authority?

- Have the necessary diagrams been provided?
- Have the necessary riser diagrams been provided?
- All equipment and fixtures scheduled?
- Does the site plan indicate the relevant location, sizes, and connections of, for example, cooling towers, fuel oil storage system, etc.?
- Are all interior exhaust fans and roof fans indicated?
- Plumbing:
  - Are the quantities and sizes provided of all equipment, fixtures, piping, special accessories, etc.?
  - Are floor and roof drains located and dimensioned?
  - Are waste line clean outs spaced per code?
  - Has the roof overflow system been correctly indicated?
  - Has a backflow preventer at the incoming water service been correctly indicated?
  - Has floor drain trap priming been clearly specified?
  - Are all valves sized and shown?
  - Have the necessary riser diagrams been provided?
  - Does the site plan indicate the relevant location, sizes, and connections of, for example, fuel oil storage system, etc.?
- Sprinkler (note: the following may apply only to the sprinkler subcontractor submission):
  - Are the quantities and sizes provided of all equipment, fixtures, piping, special accessories, etc.?
  - Do sprinkler drops and heads conflict with any other construction?
  - Have fire and jockey pump assemblies been shown and coordinated?
  - Have the necessary riser diagrams been provided?
  - Does the site plan indicate relevant location, sizes, and connections?
i. Electrical:
  - Has a layout of all the relevant electric panel and equipment rooms been provided?
  - Are the voltage and phasing requirements been shown and coordinated with those required by the manufacturers/suppliers/contractors of the mechanical systems, electrical systems, fire alarm system, security system and other special systems?
  - Do the fixture quantities differ between architectural and electrical engineering drawings?
  - Has missing device circuitry been checked for?
  - Is the required rating of the fire alarm strobe provided?

- Are all of the floor boxes indicated and accurately specified?
- Are the panels and electrical switch gear reflected in both the plan views and riser diagrams and coordinated with the other disciplines?
- Have the necessary contacts with the power and communications primary service utilities been made? Is the relevant information reflected on the contract documents? Examples: power company, telephone company, plus any specialized communications firms such as cable TV, wireless, satellite?
- Have all of the special electrical requirements been adequately shown, for example, electrified door hardware assemblies?
- Have all of the necessary empty conduit been indicated, such as conduit required for the elevator fire alarm and controls?
- Have any electrical panels been recessed into rated walls without the necessary rated protections?
- Are controls, starters and EMS protocols coordinated?

3. LIFE SAFETY
   a. General:
      - Is the design compliant with all relevant codes, standards and regulations? For example, most projects must simultaneously conform to numerous layers of federal, state and local codes and regulations plus other standards that may be included.
      - Is there adequate coordination between the owner, design professionals, contractors and the relevant governing code officials including the officials responsible for enforcing zoning, site, building, transportation, utilities, health, etc.?
      - Has all the necessary research and coordination with governing authorities, such as historic, architectural and community review boards been completed?
      - Do all of the cited standards match what is shown on the drawings or specified? For example, UL standards, FM standards, ASTM standards?
      - Has the contractor provided jurisdictional permit fees and labor?
   b. Fire separations, protections and retardancies: Are all of the following identified where applicable and in conformance with the applicable codes?
      - Wall, floor, ceiling and roof ratings?
      - Vertical egress, shaft and chase ratings?
      - Horizontal egress ratings?
      - Spray-on fireproofing and other fireproofing protections of specific elements?

- Door ratings [labels], closers, wire glass or listed fire rated glass?
- Smoke controls, such as smoke hatches, compartments?
- Correlated MEP ratings and enclosures such as at flues and exhaust stacks?
- Carpet, wall covering and drape retardancies?

   c. Discharge and paths of egress: Are all of the following vertical and horizontal discharge paths of egress efficient and clear?
- Egress loading units?
- Egress identification signs, etc.?
- Egress lighting?
- Stair and railing designs?
- Number of exits?
- Exit widths?
- Lighting?
- Dead end corridor lengths?
- Travel distances?

   d. ADA: Are all of the following in conformance with the applicable codes?
- Building entrance?
- Parking?
- Ramps?
- Vision impaired items?
- Signs?
- Toilet room clearances, stall door widths, door swing and five foot radii, plumbing fixtures?

   e. Primary utilities:
- Have all jurisdictionally adopted codes and standards of practice pertaining to primary utilities been adequately reflected?
- Has the contractor provided primary utility fees, connection fees, availability fees and labor to process been indicated?

4. INTERDISCIPLINARY COORDINATION

   a. Are the design disciplines coordinated as necessary to complete the project? Refer to geometry (dimensions, angles, radii, etc.) above, regarding systems and assemblies fitting within the available spaces.

   b. Have equipment weights, noise, vibration, heat and fumes been managed to the degree the owner anticipates?

   c. Do all the drawing backgrounds of the various disciplines match?

   d. Do all details on the drawings correspond with what has been specified and vice versa?

   e. Do the documents reflect all of the necessary trade interfaces? For example, does the electrical design provide the right voltage and phase to the right location of every mechanical device? Has all the necessary concealed blocking been provided for subsequent trades requiring it to complete their work?

f. Have all interstitial spaces, ceiling spaces, shafts, wet stacks, chase and furred spaces been properly sized to accommodate all current and future systems? Has adequate access been provided?

g. Are all of the necessary MEP hangers and supports provided?

h. Are all concealed, cast-in and imbedded items indicated and coordinated?

i. Has there been a review to verify there are no incomplete, incorrect or circular intra or interdisciplinary referencing?

100% BID SET

The bid set documents, consisting of drawings and a project manual, are used to competitively bid a project. They include all the review comments and recommendations required by the organization based on the 95% CD review. Also known as a signature set, the bid set acknowledges that the users agree with the design firm that the documents are of professional quality and are technically adequate.

In some instances the bid set may be different from the approved permit set due to unavoidable circumstances. For instance, you may have a letter or plaque indicating the building permit has been approved but the official permit set, which is signed by the building official having jurisdiction, may not have been available for delivery until the bid process has commenced. So, on occasion, you may end up with a bid set of drawings that are used by the contractor to bid the work, but will later need to build the project based on both the permit and bid set documents. If there are deviations between the two sets of documents, an addendum may be needed in order to provide clarifications between the permit and bid set documents; otherwise a change order during construction may be required.

FRONT END DOCUMENT DEVELOPMENT

Front end documents (see appendix D) are produced by the organization and given to the design firm for insertion into the project manual. It includes the invitation to bid and all the requirements for the contractor to follow regarding how the organization wants these applied and what documents must be submitted with the bid form included in the front end documents. The following is a list of items to be included in the front end documents.

Specification: Division 1 (based on Construction Specifications Institute format)
Division 01: General requirements
Section 01100: Summary
Section 01140: Work restrictions
Section 01210: Allowances
Section 01230: Alternates
Section 01270: Unit prices
Section 01290: Applications for payment
Section 01310: Project management and coordination
Section 01320: Construction progress documentation
Section 01330: Submittal procedures
Section 01350: Special procedures for projects
Section 01420: References
Section 01500: Temporary facilities and controls
Section 01600: Product requirements
Section 01710: Project commissioning for small projects
Section 01715: Full project commissioning
Section 01731: Cutting and patching
Section 01770: Project closeout
Section 01781: Project record documents
Section 01782: Operation and maintenance manuals
Section 01787: Spare parts and maintenance materials

CONTINGENT ITEMS

Contingent items are identified after review of the 95% CDs and will be incorporated into the 100% bid set and project manual. These are used to identify and mitigate risk by assigning potential quantities that are not yet known but will be needed in some amount. For example, during construction you may need to place an additional 100 tons of asphalt for wedge and leveling. If the design firm and the PM determine a potential need for an additional 150 tons of asphalt, you would simply insert a contingent line item in the project manual describing the details regarding placement of additional hot mix asphalt to pay the contractor for the additional material and labor based on the actual amount installed, without the need to generate a change order for unforeseen conditions (see appendix D, section 00200d).

6

Planning-Construction Bid Process

CONSTRUCTION ADVERTISEMENT

Working with the purchasing manager, who is the gatekeeper for this task, the PM will prepare an invitation to bid (see appendix D). The purchasing manager will review and advertise for construction work based on the 100% bid set drawings and the project manual. Public advertisement is submitted to bidding agencies that specialize in alerting customers that the project is available for bid. By referring to the sample invitation to bid, you can see how a standard invitation to bid is developed and distributed.

There are two important dates included in the invitation to bid, the bid opening/due date, and the pre-bid conference. As the PM, you will need to decide if attending a site visit will be required or strongly recommended and if it will take place immediately after the pre-bid conference or a time determined at a later date. If it is determined that a separate date is needed for a site visit, you can set one up by way of addenda at a future date and time.

The general information provided in an invitation to bid will include, at a minimum, a description of work, presentation instructions of bids indicating the submission of bid forms and any required affidavits, information on how to obtain or view documents, bid security and guarantee information, performance and payment bond information, time of completion and liquidated damages (LDs) information, pre-bid conference instructions, rules regarding award or rejection of bid information, bid protest information, construction budget information, and project administration instructions during bidding.

PRE-BID CONFERENCE AND SITE VISIT

A pre-bid conference and site visit can give you insight regarding how satis-factorily your bid documents have been prepared. For example, if you have a project budgeted for construction in the range of $3 million and you have 10 construction firms show up to the pre-bid, that is a good indication that your budget and bid documents are satisfactory. It's important to note that, even when you practice due diligence for budgets and documents, they will not be completely accurate. A contingency amount, usually around 5% to 10%, is set depending on the size of the project and if it is new construction or a renovation. In some cases, you will see renovation contingencies as high as 15% if the building is very old and contains unforeseen encapsulated or ex-posed hazardous materials such as mercury, polychlorinated biphenyls, lead, or asbestos.

A site visit is strongly recommended for a new construction project and should be mandatory for a renovation project. The site visit will help encour-age bidders to ask questions, providing an opportunity to better define the project scope of work. Corrections and revisions can be made via addenda, rather than during construction, thus reducing the risk of an RFI potentially turning into a costly change order. Do not be too discouraged if you feel that your project required several addenda because, in the scheme of the overall project, you will have saved the organization money by making sure missed or revised items are corrected during the bid process via addenda.

RFI DEVELOPMENT AND
RESPONSES DURING BIDDING

As part of the bid process, the bidders are encouraged to ask questions re-garding the bid documents. After advertisement and generally seven days prior to bid opening, the bidders can submit questions and requests for infor-mation (RFIs) to the procurement manager, who in turn will forward these to the PM who will then distribute them to the design firm for response. The responses can be general in nature or require revising or adding docu-ments or drawings. The design firm will then send the responses back to the PM, who will arrange them starting with general comments, then the project manual responses based on Construction Specifications Institute (CSI) for-matting sequences, and finally drawings, posting responses in a format se-quence of drawings outlined in the drawing index. The purchasing manager will then publish the addenda.

ADDENDA

Addenda are used to modify bid documents after they have been advertised. Bidders can provide RFIs up to seven days prior to bid opening. They can save you an enormous amount of valuable time during construction when large amounts of money are involved. Once you give a bidder a contract and notice to proceed with work, RFIs will be submitted throughout the project. Some of the RFIs will turn into additional work, thus requiring a proposed change order (PCO) from the contractor. These PCOs can be expensive because they are not priced under a competitive bidding process, not to mention any additional compensable or noncompensable time added to the project, so being able to identify and avoid the risk of change orders can be reduced by utilizing an addendum.

Once an addendum is published to the bidders, it supersedes any previously submitted information regarding those items in question. In most cases when an addendum is issued the PM will need to revise contract documents, bid forms, unit price contingent items, and allowances, and/or provide, add, or deduct alternates.

It is important that PMs post their documents with any addenda to the original drawings and specifications so that all addenda can be easily recognized in a context that will highlight these addenda.

BID OPENING

In project management the competitive sealed bidding method is preferred over a multi-step sealed bid, which allows for two phases of review, technical and price, similar to a qualifications-based selection (QBS) process but evaluating a contractor rather than a design firm. It is important to maintain a high level of due diligence in order to preserve the integrity of the process and the organization. Any hint of impropriety should be avoided.

Each invitation to bid (ITB) (see appendix D) will require every bidder to acknowledge receipt of all amendments, addenda, and changes issued. Failure on the part of a bidder to acknowledge receipt will disqualify the bidder as nonresponsive.

The contract will be awarded to the responsive and responsible bidder who meets the requirements per the ITB, based on either the most favorable bid price or most favorable evaluated bid price. Bids cannot be evaluated based on information that is not disclosed in the ITB. Bids need to be evaluated to determine which bidder offers the most favorable price to the organization per the ITB. Only objectively measurable criteria, which are described in the invitation for bids, should be applied in determining the most favorable valuated bid price. The organization needs to have the right to make the award by item, or groups of items, or total bid if it is in their best interest to do so, unless the bidder specifies in its bid that a partial or progressive award is not acceptable.

With all bids processed, the purchasing manager opens bids in public and reads the results out loud and records the costs. Contractors and the public are encouraged to attend the bid opening. If contingent items and alternates are included in the project, it is customary to also read aloud and record the cost separately. In some cases, if several bids are submitted, it may be too cumbersome to read all the individual contingent items and added or deducted alternates in detail. Cases such as these will be further evaluated to see who will be the responsive and responsible bidder. Keep in mind that the bid opening is not used to award a bidder, but merely to accept the bids for evaluation. Award recommendations will still need to be assembled based on the prospective bidder's information presented along with the bid form. It usually takes about 60 days from bid opening before the PM will have an executed contract in hand. However, the contractor is not allowed to withdraw their bid before 90 calendar days. In some cases, the contractor may be able to grant an extension of time if he feels that the numbers are still good at the time of the request.

Upon determination that the favorable bidder is both responsive and responsible, the purchasing manager will obtain all required approvals and forward the results to the PM, who concurrently will write a recommendation of award to the purchasing department. Once the recommendation is approved by the organization, the purchasing manager will coordinate the awarding of the contract to the bidder and obtain all bonding information (see appendix D). At this point, purchasing will notify the department of construction management and inspection (DCMI) to execute a purchase order (PO) assigned to the contract. It is important for the PM to verify that the bid results be available for public inspection at a reasonable time after bid opening.

If a bidder submits a favorable bid and the purchasing manager believes that a mistake was made, the bidder may be asked to confirm bid numbers for any obvious or apparent errors, especially if the bid is substantially lower than the other bids. Also, if a bidder identifies a mistake, the bidder may have the opportunity to correct or withdraw the bid based on the purchasing manager's direction. The purchasing manager determines if bid corrections or withdrawal requests are acceptable or should be denied. The purchasing manager will also determine if mistakes can be corrected after the contract is awarded.

Tie bids are bids that have the same price, terms, and conditions that meet all the requirements per the invitation for bids. Some organizations will break a tie by stating in the ITB that the award shall be made to the in-state business if identical bids are received from an in-state and an out-of-state bidder. Additionally, if a tie is between two or more in-state bidders, then some organization will award the contract to the bidder that is an in-state certified minority business enterprise (MBE). And if they are both MBE, then a drawing may need to be used to determine the winner. All of these instances need to be described in the ITB if this is the organization's policy for choosing a bid.

If a bidder is determined to be nonresponsive by the purchasing manager, that firm will be notified in writing. The purchasing manager can then offer the bidder an opportunity to explain why it was determined to be nonresponsive. Bidders can be considered nonresponsive for failure to include items in accordance with the ITB or not acknowledging any changes via addendum.

REFERENCE CHECKS

Making sure that a potential responsive general contractor has a track record for providing quality and reliable services is an important step in the award process. Before submitting a recommendation for award or sending a construction contract to the purchasing department for approval by the organization, the PM, through a written request to DCMI, needs to conduct a background check. In some organizations the PM will perform this task without help from any other agency.

In order to obtain current references, the PM will ask the contractor to provide three customer contacts and possibly one product supplier and bank with whom that the contractor has done or is doing business. By asking for a product supplier and bank reference, you can see if the contractor makes payments on time to vendors and pays bills on time. This will give you a well-vetted overall look at the solvency of the construction company and help support your recommendation for award.

Developing a reference request form is crucial to getting timely responses; making questions short and easy to answer will help. A standard list of questions may include the following:

- What did the contractor build for you?
- What was the final construction cost?
- Did the project finish on time?
- Did the subcontractors work well with the contractor?
- Was the building constructed per plan?
- Did the contractor work well with authorities having jurisdiction?
- Did the contractor submit more than 15 RFIs?
- Did any of the RFIs result in change orders?

- Were the RFIs classified as user requested, unforeseen, or error and/or omission on the designer's part?
- What was the final change order value?
- Did the contractor provide documents in a timely manner while addressing construction administration issues?
- Were any "stop work" directives issued?
- Were any lawsuits filed?
- Were there any claims?
- If so, was it resolved?
- Based on a score of 1 being the lowest and 10 being the highest, how would you score this contractor?
- Would you hire this contractor again?

When developing a list of questions, a PM should tailor them to best emphasize important issues relevant to the organization's concerns and the type of project being commissioned, being sure to ask the same questions to all the references submitted by a potential contractor who has established a responsive bid. A responsive bid is determined based on organizational purchasing rules. Typically, contractors are considered responsive by submitting all the required bid information per the bidding advertisement. Once the lowest bidder is identified the PM can then perform, or request, a reference check.

AWARD RECOMMENDATION

After reviewing the references and determining that the contractor is indeed responsive and responsible, the PM will generate an award recommendation, including the findings of the reference check that will be routed through all users having a key role in the project and then submitted to purchasing. The purchasing department later makes a recommendation to the organization for approval.

The recommendation needs to include the following:

- Sign-off by all the key stakeholders related to the project
- Provide background information, including why the project was needed
- Develop a bid tabulation of all the responsive and responsible firms
- Mention the reference check process and any relevant details
- Include budget information stating that the project is within budget

Figure 6.1 is an example of an award recommendation memo, and figures 6.2 and 6.3 are bid tabulation sheets that will be used as backup for the recommendation.

(Insert organization)

(Insert department producing this document)

(OFFICE OF PROJECT MANAGEMENT)

(Insert the address of the person responsible for the project)

TO: (purchasing, director)

THROUGH: (division of public works, director)

THROUGH: (program development & management, department head)

THROUGH: (engineering manager project management)

FROM: (project manager, Project Management)

DATE: June 1, 2006

SUBJECT: Bid Award Recommendation, Bid No. (Insert number), Anytown Fire Company

#1 Fire station

Project Account No. (Insert number)

On May 16, 2006, sealed proposals were received at the (insert organization name) purchasing department, first floor, 123 Anytown, USA for the Independent fire company #1 fire station project. The proposals were opened and publicly read at 3:00 p.m. Five (5) firms submitted a proposal (see attached bid tabulation sheet).

The Anytown Fire Company #1Fire Station, which is part of Hometown Volunteer Fire Company, is located at 123 main street, hometown, USA and owned by the Hometown Volunteer Fire Company. A new station is being proposed to be built on ground owned by the Fire Company located at 2nd. Street. The current building, which was built in 1887, is too small for the current needs of the Fire Company. This project would build a new 5 bay station and administrative areas in accordance with the previously developed fire station program developed and used for all fire stations. The company is requesting approximately 17,000 square feet for the fire station.

The base bid for this construction project is for a 17,000 sqft fire station that includes:

- Site improvements to connect to existing egress and entrances.
- Approximately 8,600 sqft of bunk rooms, lockers and showers, storage, and administrative

Figure 6.1.1

- Approximately 8,400 sqft of apparatus bays. The five equal bays have been designed for pull-through capability of the apparatus.

Six alternates were also requested from responding firms. During the bid process, alternate #1 for insulated roof and wall panels in lieu of blanket insulation was added to the base bid, and therefore no pricing for this alternate was received. The remaining five alternates are as follows:

Alternate #2 – Firehouse flooring and striping in lieu of epoxy
Alternate #3 – An overhead vehicle exhaust system
Alternate #4 – Expanded concrete apron at front bays to reduce impact loading
Alternate #5 – Upgrade of seven overhead door controls
Alternate #6 – Site sign with lighting

DCMI has conducted an evaluation of the lowest bidder, contractor Bidder #5 of anytown, USA as a part of the bid process. This evaluation included a review of the bidder's project experience and reference verification, and determined that Bidder #5are a responsive and responsible bidder. Attached to this award recommendation is the contractor evaluation completed by DCMI.

Staff recommends awarding the construction contract for the independent fire company #1 fire station project (Bid No. (insert number) to Bidder #5, the lowest responsive and responsible bidder, in the amount of $2,578,406.50, which includes the base bid amount of $2,391,738.00 for a 210-day construction duration, alternates #2, #3, #4, and #6, in the amount of $151,848.00, a contingency allowances of $6,000 for additional soil testing, and unit price contingent items of $28,820.50. With a recommended construction contingency of 5% or $128,920.33, the funds required to sufficiently fund this project for construction total $2,714,112.10.

Funding for the award of this contract will come from one source, Capital Project (Insert number) in the amount of $2,714,112.10.

FUNDING INFORMATION:

Budget Implications: No_____   Yes__X____
(If yes, provide the necessary information as outlined below.)

Name of Accounts: Anytown Fire Company #1 Fire Station Project.

Account Numbers: (insert project construction account number)

Figure 6.1.2

Office of Project Management Bid: #(Insert Number): Anytown Fire Company #1 Opening Date: (Insert Date)at 3:00 PM Local Time Document preparer: (Insert PM) Project Manager Office of Project Management	bidder #1	Bidder #2	Bidder #3	Bidder #4	Bidder #5
Total Base Bid:	$2,695,000.00	$2,550,000.00	$2,590,000.00	$2,719,000.00	$2,391,738.00
Add Alternate #1 Not Used- moved to base bid Insulated panels	N/A	N/A	N/A	N/A	N/A
Add Alternate #2 Firehouse floor in lieu of epoxy	$7,380.00	$28,500.00	$13,529.00	$6,236.00	$8,200.00
Add Alternate #3 Overhead Vehicle Exhaust System	$106,400.00	$99,928.00	$126,621.00	$99,687.00	$106,775.00
Add Alternate #4 Expanded Concrete apron in front of bays	$9,500.00	$5,000.00	$15,566.00	$7,600.00	$12,255.00
Deduct Alternate #5 Anytown Fire Company #1 Station 22-Door Control Upgrades ((NOT ACCEPTED))	-$21,000.00	-$19,000.00	-$26,140.00	-$3,500.00	-$22,800.00
Add Alternate #6 Site Sign with Lighting	$19,200.00	$18,500.00	$25,008.00	$11,000.00	$24,618.00
Allowance #1 Testing for soils	$6,000.00	$6,000.00	$6,000.00	$6,000.00	$6,000.00
Total Cost of Alternates + Allowances:	$148,480.00	$157,928.00	$186,724.00	$130,523.00	$157,848.00
Total Cost of Unit Price Contingent Items (see Page 2 for detail):	$37,065.00	$24,975.00	$40,013.60	$44,875.00	$28,820.50
Total Base Bid, plus Alternates, plus Total Contingent Items:	$2,880,545.00	$2,732,903.00	$2,816,737.60	$2,894,398.00	$2,578,406.50

Alternate descriptions

Alternate #1: This alternate was for providing insulated structural roof and wall panels and associated trim, including gutters, downspouts, and fasteners in lieu of comparable metal building components. During the bidding phase, we decided that these items needed to be provided in the base bid as was done at Anytown Fire Company #1 Station 22.

Alternate #2: This alternate would provide the firehouse floor system and striping in lieu of epoxy flooring and will create a safer environment for the firemen to operate in the bay by providing better footing with less chance of slipping.

Alternate #3: Provide Overhead vehicle exhaust system in apparatus bays. DFRS is requesting this item be added due to codes that will require them in the future. If we do this work under this contract, it will cost less than waiting to retrofit this station later on.

Alternate #4: Provide expanded concrete apron in front of apparatus bays- this alternate is being requested to help reduce the impact loading on the pavement at the bay doors thus helping reduce costly pavement repairs in the future.

Deduct Alternate #5: Replacement of seven (7) overhead door controls at Anytown Fire Company #1 Station 22- As part of our lessons learned, we would like to request that this alternate NOT be accepted so that the door controls can be upgraded by replacing the existing relay systems with solid state logic control boards, including remote controls. This upgrade will help eliminate potential problems when responding to calls. It will make the door controls more reliable and thus will help in emergency response time.

Add Alternate #6: Site Sign and associated lighting- DFRS is requesting approval of this sign to help the public identify the building. If accepted, a plan review at staff level will be required to approve the sign lighting.

Figure 6.2

CONTINGENT ITEMS

Company

#	Contingent Item descriptions	Per	QTY	1		2		3		4		5	
				Unit price	sub total	Unit price	sub total	Unit price	sub total	Unit price	sub total	Unit price	sub total
1	Earth Excavation - Machine	C.Y.	15	$16.00	$240.00	$10.00	$150.00	$9.80	$147.00	$15.00	$225.00	$16.50	$247.50
2	Earth Excavation - Hand	C.Y.	5	$115.00	$575.00	$115.00	$575.00	$36.75	$183.75	$85.00	$425.00	$110.00	$550.00
3	Trench Excavation & Haul Off-Site	C.Y.	5	$25.00	$125.00	$24.00	$120.00	$17.15	$85.75	$55.00	$275.00	$24.50	$122.50
4	Trench Rock Excavation & Haul Off Site	C.Y.	5	$105.00	$525.00	$85.00	$425.00	$42.87	$214.35	$150.00	$750.00	$101.00	$505.00
5	Remove Unsuitable Soils & Haul Off Site	C.Y.	5	$70.00	$350.00	$65.00	$325.00	$42.87	$214.35	$150.00	$750.00	$71.00	$355.00
6	Structural Fill form Off-Site +	C.Y.	10	$20.00	$200.00	$19.00	$190.00	$19.60	$196.00	$45.00	$450.00	$21.50	$215.00
7	Placement & Compaction (95%)	C.Y.	20	$21.00	$420.00	$19.00	$380.00	$34.30	$686.00	$45.00	$900.00	$23.15	$463.00
8	Permanent Seeding and Mulch	S.Y.	10	$2.00	$20.00	$2.00	$20.00	$1.22	$12.20	$10.00	$100.00	$245.00	$2,450.00
9	Temporary Seeding and Mulch	S.Y.	10	$1.00	$10.00	$1.00	$10.00	$0.98	$9.80	$10.00	$100.00	$1.25	$12.50
10	Concrete Sidewalk	S.F.	50	$5.00	$250.00	$3.00	$150.00	$5.94	$297.00	$6.00	$300.00	$3.65	$182.50
11	Unreinforced Concrete Fill	C.Y.	10	$100.00	$1,000.00	$190.00	$1,900.00	$137.72	$1,377.20	$220.00	$2,200.00	$125.00	$1,250.00
12	Reinforced Concrete Including Formwork, Finishing and reinforcing	C.Y.	10	$300.00	$3,000.00	$240.00	$2,400.00	$661.50	$6,615.00	$400.00	$4,000.00	$140.00	$1,400.00
13	120 Volt Duplex Receptacle, Raceway, wiring and Breaker on a Dedicated Circuit	each	10	$160.00	$1,600.00	$285.00	$2,850.00	$612.42	$6,124.20	$155.00	$1,550.00	$195.00	$1,950.00
14	120 Volt Duplex Receptacle & Wiring, Connected to a Local Receptacle Branch Circuit	each	10	$130.00	$1,300.00	$85.00	$850.00	$196.00	$1,960.00	$110.00	$1,100.00	$155.00	$1,550.00
15	20 Amp Light Switch, Connecte to Lights being Controlled	each	10	$130.00	$1,300.00	$85.00	$850.00	$196.00	$1,960.00	$110.00	$1,100.00	$135.00	$1,350.00
16	Data/Tele. Outlet, including box,	each	10	$100.00	$1,000.00	$38.00	$380.00	$150.00	$1,500.00	$60.00	$600.00	$80.00	$800.00
17	Exit Sign	each	10	$250.00	$2,500.00	$235.00	$2,350.00	$230.00	$2,300.00	$250.00	$2,500.00	$250.00	$2,500.00
18	Fire Alarm System A/V device	each	10	$650.00	$6,500.00	$290.00	$2,900.00	$345.00	$3,450.00	$400.00	$4,000.00	$345.00	$3,450.00
19	Fire Alarm Horn Modules	each	5	$580.00	$2,900.00	$300.00	$1,500.00	$345.00	$1,725.00	$350.00	$1,750.00	$175.00	$875.00
20	Emergency lighting battery unit	each	10	$270.00	$2,700.00	$50.00	$500.00	$375.00	$3,750.00	$350.00	$3,500.00	$340.00	$3,400.00
21	Card Reader Door Control	each	10	$1,040.00	$10,400.00	$600.00	$6,000.00	$690.00	$6,900.00	$1,800.00	$18,000.00	$505.00	$5,050.00
22	MDSCD Silt Fence	L.F.	50	$3.00	$150.00	$3.00	$150.00	$6.12	$306.00	$6.00	$300.00	$2.85	$142.50
	Totals of Contingent Items:				$37,065.00		$24,975.00		$40,013.60		$44,875.00		$28,820.50

Figure 6.3

7

Construction

PROJECT HAND-OFF

Because construction management is a career field unto itself and requires an extensive amount of information, I elected to introduce some of the dynamics of construction management as it pertains to the interactions that bridge PM and CM activities.

Upon organization approval of the award recommendation, a purchasing department will proceed with gathering all the required bonding and insurance information per the instructions in the project manual. Because the construction manager (CM) is the gatekeeper of the construction contract, the PM will coordinate with CM to expedite the construction work.

After receiving confirmation from purchasing that the contractor's bonding and insurance has been established, CM administration can assign and execute a purchase order (PO). POs allow the organization to encumber funds that are established during the CIP process and lock in the funding. This will help reduce the potential risk of other billings inadvertently being applied to the fund balance in the construction account. Using figure 6.1 as an example, we execute a contract in the amount of $2,578,406.50 (once a PO is executed, these funds will become an encumbered amount). Let's assume the original funds are $2,580,000.00 assigned to the construction account and $13,000.00 in the interagency information technologies (IIT) department account. Knowing that IIT has sole ownership of the $13,000.00, it is assumed that any IIT costs incurred on the project will be assigned to this account. During project construction, IIT uses up its $13,000.00 but still needs to bill $2,000.00 for additional unforeseen wire installations, and someone inadvertently charges this to the construction account rather than the IIT account. Because you only have an unencumbered amount of $1,593.50, which is the amount left over when subtracting the budgeted and actual construction account funds ($2,580,000.00 – $2,578,406.59), the construction account ends up with a deficit of $406.50 ($1,593.50 – $2,000.00). Since construction funds have already been earmarked/encumbered, the deficit will not affect the encumbered construction funds but will affect the unencumbered funds. Now how do we address the deficit in the unencumbered construction account funds? Some organizations will keep the construction account balance negative and assess the deficit to the overall project budget; as long as the overall project budget does not go negative, and the discrepancy is a small amount, the budget department may want us to track those differences internally to the project. But technically, you would need to request a budget amendment that will increase the construction account by $406.50 in order to keep the construction account balanced. It is important to know that in this cost-conscious environment, the first option may be a viable one. It would eliminate the internal labor cost required to process such a small amount; in fact, the internal labor cost involved may end up costing the organization more than $2,000.00 to process it, so keeping track of these deficits and credits within the project accounts and recording them as part of a project status report can provide the same result while saving the organization a substantial amount of internal labor costs.

Let us dissect how funds are assigned to a project during the CIP process. When the CIP committee reviews and recommends approval, a project is assigned an overall project budget based on a breakdown of accounts within the overall project. These accounts may be assigned as follows:

- Site account: Established to pay for funds related to utilities, permit, tap, and printing fees.
- Architect/engineering account: Established to pay for design firm services, this is the account where the design firm's PO, awarded via the RFP process, resides. Invoices received against the project will be deducted from this PO. Having the design firm include the PO number on the invoice is important for the processing of payments in a timely fashion.
- Construction account: As with the architect/engineer account, this is established so that a PO can be established for the construction work and the contractor can invoice against the established PO.
- Inspections: The CM may assign an inspector and administrator to a construction project that requires administrative support. The amount allocated

is established during the CIP process via a recommended funding level by the division director.

- Equipment account: Equipment funds are required based on the user's need for furnishings. Organizations develop rules that will help identify what is equipment versus what is a furnishing. In my organization, furnishings are classified as any items that are not required to be mechanically fastened down in some manner in order for it to function. For example, a sofa, desk, modular office furniture, or conference table and chair are rarely mechanically fastened to building components. But there is a gray area; for instance, the project program may call for a high-end residential refrigerator with an ice-maker and water dispenser. Because the refrigerator needs rough-in plumbing provided and installed by the general contractor, it is more beneficial to have the contractor provide and install the refrigerator complete. This would provide the advantage of getting the best price for the refrigerator through the bid process rather than sole-sourcing the refrigerator and paying for the extras that the contractor would include, such as delivery, set-up, and clean-up. This also works well when the project requires a washer and dryer. Keep in mind that commercial equipment is always considered part of the construction contract and not the equipment account, due to all the special health department requirements and inspections.
- IIT account: Most organizations have a need for communication connectivity for computers, data services, phones, and remote monitoring. This is the account that will include components necessary for operating these types of services. For example, additional phone lines, data jacks and racks, generator monitoring, access system monitoring, and closed-circuit television (CCTV) equipment are assigned to this account. Any rough-in requirements, such as single gang boxes, conduit stubbed above or below with a pull string, or preparing a centralized equipment location, is included in the construction account. A general rule of thumb is that IIT will run their own wire, install their own devices, and service this equipment. Everything required to support these items will need to be part of the construction contract. It is important to establish a clear division between what is provided in-house and what the contractor is obligated to provide. For instance, our organization mandates that any IIT equipment rooms maintain a maximum temperature of 75 degrees. So we need to make sure that the design firm is aware of this and provides an economical way of meeting this requirement. It could mean that spot cooling or a vented door is provided and installed by the contractor.
- Project management account: As with CM assigning an inspector and administrator, this account is funded during CIP via a recommended funding

level by the division director and/or the PMO. This is the account that PMs will use to charge their time.

It is important to know that budgeted project funds are different from actual funds assigned to individual project accounts. Budgeted funds are established by the CIP committee for the overall project, and actual funds required are distributed among the project accounts, and you essentially lock in the money so that it is solely available for use in the designated established project accounts. For example, you have $3,500.00 assigned to the site account and are showing a negative balance of, say, -$300.00 in the PM account. You cannot use the $3,500.00 to balance the PM account because the entire $3,500.00 has already been encumbered. You would have to request unencumbered funds in the amount of $300.00 to balance the PM account via a budget transfer request. The budget transfer request option is used when the overall project funds have additional money in an account that may have been assigned as a contingency amount, that is, encumbered funds that are no longer needed for that particular account to finish the project. For example, you may have an encumbered amount of $3,500.00 in the site account. Due to a reduction in services, the account has a positive final fund balance of $500.00. Using a budget transfer request, you can ask the budget department to unencumber the positive balance and apply or re-encumber the balance to another account that needs additional funds.

PRE-CONSTRUCTION MEETING

Before a pre-construction meeting takes place it is important to make sure that all permits have been approved. The CM and the PM need to verify that all required permits are in order. This will allow the contractor to apply for any required contractor permits that will be generated based on the approved building, and site permits thus eliminating any potential prolonged work stoppages. Once the contractor provides a schedule of values and the CM approves and records this so that invoices can be processed against the PO established in the construction account and based on actual work completed, CM will set up a meeting with the contractor, their subcontractors, PM, design firm, and their subcontractors. The CM inspector will forward an agenda to the PM who will distribute it to the project users, design firm, and/or purchasing.

The meeting will be run by the CM inspector assigned to the project and will provide information relevant to starting work. Using the following checklist, items to be discussed should include:

Heading information:

- ☐ Project name
- ☐ Bid number
- ☐ Meeting minutes number

- ☐ Meeting date
- ☐ Attendees list, including name and company

General contract information:

- ☐ Contract duration
- ☐ Notice to proceed with construction
- ☐ Time used
- ☐ Time remaining
- ☐ Weather days used
- ☐ Percent completed
- ☐ Original finish date
- ☐ Revised finish date
- ☐ RFIs submitted
- ☐ RFIs resolved
- ☐ RFIs open

- ☐ Change orders and status
- ☐ Submittals not processed
- ☐ Bond and insurance active dates
- ☐ Date building permits turned over to CM
- ☐ Working hours
- ☐ Preliminary submittal log—date approved by CM
- ☐ Construction progress for last two weeks
- ☐ Construction progress projected for next two weeks

Business items:

- ☐ New business items
- ☐ Old business items

- ☐ Outstanding business items

With the preconstruction meeting complete, the construction inspector will distribute meeting minutes to all attendees and will proceed to lay the groundwork and coordination required to have the job site ready for groundbreaking. This can take some time depending on the size of the project. Using the fire station example, we can assume three weeks before clearing and grubbing the site can begin. During this time, the contractor will be installing soil conservation measures, that is, silt fence and stabilized construction entrances, construction trailers, and surveying horizontal and vertical controls for site and building layout, metes and bounds, and utility layouts. Once these items are approved by the inspector having jurisdiction, the contractor can then start foundation work. Any questions or RFIs from the contractor are routed to the architect via the construction inspector and/or project manager respectively for responses and proper record keeping.

SUBMITTALS

Once a construction notice to proceed is issued, the contractor will start submitting shop drawings, cut sheets, and material submissions to the design firm for review based on an approved submittal log. The log is developed by the contractor for review and approval by the construction inspector and design firm. Submittals are typically lumped into packages that end up being submitted sporadically throughout construction; for example, the design firm may receive one package for all the plumbing fixtures, pipe, and fittings as one submission. Once approved by the design firm, the construction inspector will document the status of the submittal in the log by indicating approval, rejection, resubmission, or approved as noted, and then recording the date.

It is important to note that submittals are directly related to the construction schedule in that different material will require different lead time; hence the sporadic submissions. For example, if the plumbing fixtures are approved in the submittal log, and are clearly off-the-shelf items, you could expect them to be on site and ready for install within 7 to 10 days. However, if the submittal was approved early on, then the contractor would wait to deliver the approved material until it is needed per the approved construction schedule. If the approved submittal is for a specialty item, such as a 600 kilowatt generator, manufacture time may be as long as nine weeks before the item is scheduled for delivery. Reviewing the submittal log on a regular basis will identify which items will require a long or short lead time and how they affect current or future work activities outlined in the construction schedule.

It is in the project's best interest to start the submittals for long lead time items as soon as possible to avoid any delays on the project.

As an additional PM task, you will need to verify that proper material types, accessories, and color choices have been approved and ordered per the user's choices during the 95% CD process. These tasks will help identify and mitigate some risk that could potentially delay the project, which would translate into additional cost.

SCHEDULE OF VALUES (SOV)

As with submittals, a schedule of values (SOV) is developed and submitted by the contractor for review and approval by the design firm and construction inspector after the pre-construction meeting but before start of construction. All payment requisitions (see appendix F) will be developed and paid based on the approved SOV and used to validate progress payment requests. The SOV is another tool used by a PM to review project progress and track cost.

Used in conjunction with the submittal log, a PM can review the overall project performance and identify areas of needed improvement in order to finish the project on time and within budget.

RFIs IN CONSTRUCTION

In construction, as in design, it is understood that no project is perfect. For all the risks you identify and avoid, some items, hopefully not catastrophic, will be missed.

During construction, contractors will ask questions related to unclear design requirements. If direction on the design conflicts with conditions at the site, the contactor will identify and describe the issues to the construction inspector, and if they cannot agree on what the designer intended the contractor will provide a written request for information (RFI) to the design firm for direction on how to proceed with construction. If that direction indicates additional construction materials and labor above the original project requirements, then the PM will request a proposed change order (PCO), or request for tender (RFT), through the construction inspector who will then forward that request to the contractor. After the contractor prepares the PCO/RFT including a detailed breakdown of time and material, the construction inspector will review the price for fairness and accuracy. Once the construction inspector is satisfied with the document, he will forward it to the design firm and PM for review and recommendation. If approved, a change order (CO) will then be generated, processed, and approved for the work identified. It is important to understand that the construction inspector is the gatekeeper for processing RFIs. He or she will have a tracking system in place that will keep all these requests in some sort of order. The construction inspector governs how RFIs will be assigned, and records the result. An RFI could be answered without any costs associated with the direction, or it could end up turning into a PCO and then a CO.

CHANGE ORDERS (COs)

As part of the construction inspector's gatekeeping responsibilities, change orders (see appendix G) need to be processed in a timely and efficient manner because change orders are directly related to time and money. In construction management there are specific steps required to get to a finalized change order. As described in the RFI section, an RFI is the catalyst for the change management process. Once a PCO is provided to the construction inspector, they will go through the following steps before moving on to the approval process.

- Estimated cost: The construction inspector works with the contractor to provide a rough estimate of cost and time.
- Quoted cost: The contractor provides a PCO to the construction inspector for review.
- Negotiated cost: The contractor and construction inspector investigate a detailed breakdown of time and material (T&M) to verify that the PCO is fair. In the event that an agreement cannot be reached, a construction change directive (CCD)/work change directive (WCD) (see appendix H) can be issued according to the general conditions of the construction contract. This may be the only option when a project is in construction and needs to move forward with the least amount of impact on the construction schedule.
- Final cost: Assuming that a CCD/WCD has not been issued, and once consensus is established between the contractor, construction inspector, design firm, and PM, a change order can be processed for execution.

Using these steps as part of your quality assurance/quality control process (QA/QC) will help ensure that the change has been thoroughly scrutinized and delivered in a timely/quality manner before approval. In addition, the PM will need to verify justification for the CO and who originated the change; review any potential problems and workaround solutions, benefits realized and detriments realized by the change; and decide if an order-of-magnitude estimate by the design firm is required along with the firm's review and recommendation of the PCO.

Once the construction inspector is in agreement with the price, and approval from the design firm and PM is recommended, he will proceed with processing a change order for the organization's upper management, based on the organization's change order policies.

It is widely accepted in the construction and design industry that change orders are a given for almost all projects, and more so for big projects. A few items that may generate the need for a change order could be a discovery of unforeseen conditions, any deviations from the original design, and extensions of time due to changes out of the contractor's control such as user-requested changes and errors and/or omissions (E&Os) by the design firm.

Another factor that drives a change order is how the orders are approved. Because time is of the essence, organizations provide or develop a change order policy that describes how these are processed. For instance, as with design, a construction change order will be identified as a user-requested, unforeseen condition, error and/or omission, or a balancing change order. Cost also affects how long it will take to process a change order; cost is directly related to the level of approval authority held by upper management. In our organization, we have upset limits that determine approval authority as follows:

CEO/organizational approval required for:
- Any change order that is equal to or more than 15% of the original bid award amount
- Any change order over $50,000

CFO/county manager approval required for:
- Any change order over $25,000.00 up to $50,000.00

Director for:
- Any change order up to $25,000.00

Construction manager for:
- Any contingent items, set up as a pre-approved change order amount with the fee not to exceed the pre-approved amount, in the contract used as specified

Beware that, in some small instances, you may run across an excessively low bidder who is exploiting an opportunity to get the work knowing that they can add change orders for items once the contract has been executed. By checking references and work histories, you should be able to minimize this risk.

Documentation and tracking change orders are a critical part of what PMs do during project construction. Figure 7.1 is an example of a change order summary log used to verify budget information at a glance, which affords the PM the ability to forecast project fund balances and potential funds required for change orders that may be needed in the future. Budget adjustments can then be made to keep funds in a positive fund balance.

COST MANAGEMENT

In order to control budgeted CIP project funds, PMs employ cost-control measures to anticipate any changes in cost. The following formulas based on earned value management techniques (EVM) will help evaluate the fiscal health of your project as it progresses.

- Budget at completion (BAC): Represents the amount of funds left at the end of a project (BAC = total PV at completion). Essentially, it is the budgeted cost originally planned for a project. For example:

Contractor: Bidder #5
Bid No. (Insert Number)
Project Number: (Insert Number)
PO Number: (Insert Number)
Original contract duration: 210 days
Date of NTP: (Insert Date)

Original Contract PO Amount:	$2,578,406.50		
Original construction account Budget Balance:		$2,707,235.93	
Change order total & % from CO#1 thru CO# 26;		($34,517.26)	1.339%
Current contract increased amount:		$2,543,889.24	

Original completion date: 05-30-2007
Revised completion date as of progress meeting # 19:

Change order types :	QTY.	CO cost	% of overall cost	
E&O's	5	($13,865.23)	-0.538%	
User Requested	5	$805.45	0.031%	Total
Unforeseen conditions	15	($48,989.98)	-1.900%	-1.390%
Administrative	1	$27,532.50	1.02%	

E&O's potential fees to date: $1,301.00

CO #	Change order description	CO Type	E&O fee	Non-comp days added	CO unit cost	budget balance
1	Oil Separator	unforeseen	$0.00	0	($5,094.92)	$128,828.50
2	Weather Delays	unforeseen	$0.00	2	$0.00	$128,828.50
3	Additional steel angle	user request	$0.00	0	($1,006.25)	$127,822.25
4	ERV modifications	unforeseen	$0.00	0	($13,113.82)	$114,708.43
5	Weather Delays	unforeseen	$0.00	3	$0.00	$114,708.43
6	Security system credit	user request	$0.00	0	$13,513.50	$128,221.93
7	Front entry structure	unforeseen	$0.00	0	($1,290.00)	$126,931.93
8	Sign change	user request	$0.00	0	($1,987.00)	$124,944.93
9	Backflow preventers	Error on A/E	$713.00	0	($7,134.03)	$117,810.90
10	Best door hardware	unforeseen	$0.00	0	($10,886.92)	$106,923.98
11	Building sign changes	unforeseen	$0.00	0	($7,589.16)	$99,334.82
12	Revised Sink	Error on A/E	$84.00	0	($845.20)	$98,489.62
13	Additional Emg. Lighting	user request	$0.00	0	($2,454.84)	$96,034.78
14	Opticon system	user request	$0.00	0	($7,259.96)	$88,774.82
15	Alm. Hatch covers	unforeseen	$0.00	0	($3,019.02)	$85,755.80
16	Stove upgrade	unforeseen	$0.00	0	($349.00)	$85,406.80
17	Railing change door #2	unforeseen	$0.00	0	($1,226.28)	$84,180.52
18	Additional fire land stripping	unforeseen	$0.00	0	($1,604.61)	$82,575.91
19	HVAC manual shut-down	Error on A/E	$174.00	0	($1,744.20)	$80,831.71
20	Add smoke damper	Error on A/E	$296.00	0	($2,959.20)	$77,872.51
21	120V circuit install	Error on A/E	$118.00	0	($1,182.60)	$76,689.91
22	Add'l fire extinguisher	unforeseen	$0.00	0	($173.25)	$76,516.66
23	Remote test switch for ERV	unforeseen	$0.00	0	($759.40)	$75,757.26
24	Subgrade repair	unforeseen	$0.00	0	($1,791.60)	$73,965.66
25	overhead door jamb ext.	unforeseen	$0.00	0	($2,092.00)	$71,873.66
26	balancing CO	admin	$0.00	0	$27,532.50	$99,406.16

Figure 7.1

- You have a paving project that requires 5,000 square feet of pavement at a predicted total cost of $10,500.00, and should take 72 hours to complete. BAC would = $10,500.00.
- Planned value (PV): Represents the budgeted cost for work scheduled (BCWS) to be completed on an activity or WBS totaling the entire project for a specified point in time. This cost is determined during the CIP development phase (planned percent completed × BAC). Using the example above, we can do the following:
  - You would like to see what the PV is at 10 hours into the work. Using the formula we can determine that 10 hours ÷ 72 hours is 13.89% of the overall time used, so PV = 13.89% × $10,500.00. Thus PV = $1,458.45 at 10 hours.
- Earned value (EV): Represents the budgeted amount for the work actually completed (BWAC) at a point in time on the schedule. It allows a PM to see the actual work completed at that point (actual percent complete × BAC). For example:
  - You are 30 hours into the paving project and need to see if the project is progressing according to the original budget amount. Knowing 30 hours ÷ 72 hours is 41.67% of the overall time used, we can calculate EV = 41.67% × $10,500.00. Thus EV = $5,005.35 of value earned for the project.
- Actual cost (AC): Also known as the actual cost of work performed (ACWP), this represents the total cost incurred at a point in time in a project schedule. For instance:
  - You need to know if the costs incurred at 62 hours into the project are accurate. Assume 62 hours into the project you have spent $9,041.67. Using the formula AC = BAC ÷ 72 hours × 62, then AC = $10,500.00 ÷ 72 hours × 62 hours = $9,041.67. This verifies the actual cost to date.

The PV, EV, and AC are used to provide forecasts that allow the PM to determine if the project is performing or not performing based on the original budget at any point in the project's timeline. As part of the system to forecast costs and schedules during points along the projected schedule of a project and its projected cost, PV, EV, and AC can be identified at any point during a project, allowing for calculations that can be shown graphically as s-curves of cost variance, schedule variance, cost performance index, and schedule performance index to determine project performance regarding budgeted costs and schedules:

- Cost variance (CV): Shows the difference between budget at completion (BAC) of the project and the actual cost (CV = EV − AC). An example would be as follows:

- Using our pavement project example, say we have an AC of $10,400.00 and an EV of $10,500.00 at the end of the project, meaning the end of 72 hours. So using the formula CV = $10,500.00 − $10,400.00, CV = $100.00, indicating that our project showed the cost to be less than predicted.
- Schedule variance (SV): Compares when the project was completed to the actual completion time/original duration. SV will ultimately equal zero when the project is complete based on all PVs being completed (SV = EV − PV).
  - We can see what the SV is 30 hours into the project, assuming an EV of $4,000.00. SV = 4,000.00 − 30 hours ÷ 72 hours × $10,500.00. Thus SV= 4,000.00 − 4,375.00, thus SV = -$375.00. This negative amount shows that the project is underperforming regarding schedule. Had SV been a positive amount, the project would have been performing ahead of schedule. If it were zero, then the project would have been performing as scheduled.
- Cost performance index (CPI): Determines if the project is showing a cost overrun, that is, less than 1 represents underperformance, 1 means precisely performing as predicted, and greater than 1 represents the project performing better than expected at any point during the project (CPI = EV ÷ AC). As an example:
  - The paving project is running an EV of $5,005.35 after 30 hours of work. Let's assume that at 30 hours of work we have an AC of 5,000.00. The formula is CPI = $5,005.35 ÷ $5,000.00, thus CPI = 1.001 indicating that the project is performing slightly above average. Basically this means that for every dollar put in, the project is earning a value of $1.001.
- Schedule performance index (SPI): Helps forecast a project completion date and, when used in conjunction with CPI, will help provide completion estimates. The same principle applies to SPI as for CPI: if less than 1 then the project is behind schedule, if precisely 1 then the project is performing according to the projected schedule, if greater than 1 then the project is performing better than the expected schedule (SPI = EV ÷ PV). As an example:
  - Let's assume that 25 hours have elapsed for the paving project and the EV is $3,000.00. PV would be $3,645.83. Using the formula SPI = $3,000.00 ÷ $3,645.83, then SPI = 0.823, indicating that the project is not progressing as it should.

When a project proceeds along the developed timeline, the PM can employ the earned value technique (EVT) to forecast estimates or predictions based on current or future events by inputting BAC, AC to date, and CPI to calculate estimate at completion, estimate to complete, and variance at completion.

- Estimate at completion (EAC): Forecasts performance at a precise point in time related to the project's BAC and CPI (EAC = BAC ÷ CPI). Let's assume that the paving project has a BAC of $10,500.00 and a CPI of 1.001, then EAC = $10,500.00 ÷ 1.09 = 9,633.03. This shows us that we are performing better than expected regarding cost, because we expected to spend $10,500.00 and only spent $9,633.03.
- Estimate to complete (ETC): Forecasts the amount needed to finish the work (ETC = EAC − AC).
  - Again using the pavement example, assume an EAC of $9,633.03 and an AC of $10,500.00. Using the formula, ETC = $9,633.03 − $10,500.00, thus ETC = -$866.97, showing that the project is performing better than expected regarding cost and no additional funds are required to finish the work.
- Variance at completion (VAC): Represents the difference between the original established funding amount and the actual amount expected to finish the project (VAC = BAC − EAC). For instance:
  - For the pavement project, we see that BAC = $10,500.00 and assume an EAC of $9,500.00. Using the formula we can see that VAC = $10,500.00 − $9,500.00, thus VAC = $1,000.00. Since this number is positive, the project is doing better than expected. If it were a negative number, the project would be showing a cost overrun.
- To-complete performance index (TCPI): Represents the future CPI required to meet a project's intended costs based on the work needed to finish the project (TCPI = BAC − EV ÷ EAC − AC). Using the following example we can see how TCPI is calculated:
  - Assume that the paving project is 30 hours into the work and the PM notices that the original BAC is not achievable. The PM will need to develop a new EAC, which becomes the new BAC, say $12,000.00. Based on an EV of $4,000.00 and an AC of $6,900.00, TCPI = $12,000.00 − $4,000.00 ÷ $12,000.00 − $6,900.00, so TCPI = $8,000.00 ÷ $5,100.00 and thus TCPI = 1.57. To meet the new ETC, the project must perform at or greater than 1.57 in order to be successfully completed.

SUBSTANTIAL COMPLETION

As the project starts to wind down and work gets closer to completion, and a use and occupancy (U&O) or temporary U&O has been issued by the jurisdiction having authority, the organization's inspector will inform the design firm and the PM that substantial completion documents are in progress and will require review and comments before issuing the substantial completion document (see appendix I). Included as part of the document is a final punch list document, along with issuance of a U&O or temporary U&O, which will allow the organization to start using the building for its intended use while allowing the contractor to reduce their retainage and finish the punch list items.

The substantial completion form will also include acceptance by the contractor as conditions for completing the contract. They include the final punch list, turning over all product and maintenance user manuals, warranty information, and any labor warranty agreements.

USE AND OCCUPANCY (U&O)

A U&O permit is a big milestone for the organization. Internal agencies will need to coordinate items such as furnishings in order to operate. However, until a U&O is established, no furnishings can be set up in the facility. As a double-edged sword, after furnishings are installed an unforeseen life safety issue may be generated by the placement of some furnishings. For instance, a library has open floor space that has been approved for U&O, but after installing the stacks, the fire marshal notices that a sprinkler head and a wall-mounted audio/visual fire alarm device is obstructed. Due to these items being a life safety issue, the fire marshal can place a hold on the U&O and require that these items be fixed before further fit-out can commence. To avoid this, our organization uses ceiling-mounted audio/visual fire alarm devices and flexible head sprinklers, which allows the contractor the ability to relocate those items with little effort. Hard-piped sprinklers would require a day or two to relocate and wall-mounted audio/visual devices may require three to four days to relocate, not to mention needing to place a blank cover over a useless device box.

PUNCH LIST

As part of the substantial completion requirements, a punch list is developed so the contractor can have an organized list of items requiring repair or completion as intended in the specifications of the project.

When performing a walk-through, it is good to inform users not familiar with the process that flaws are expected. Since people perceive what a flaw is in very different ways, it is impossible to provide a baseline list of unacceptable flaws based on a single person's description. Because of this, acceptable flaws can be described as flaws that are considered to be within industry tolerances and/or standards. Remember that all facilities will have flaws. Unacceptable flaws are flaws that require some repair or reinstallation, or in some cases an item may be missing.

Items on the list must be incidental and the list cannot include items that will not allow the organization to use the space. More times than not, the organization will have a combined punch list that includes comments from the construction inspector, facility users, PM, and maintenance. Working with the construction inspector, the PM will gather all the comments from the users and combine them into one document that is then provided to the construction inspector, who then adds the other comments and includes the documents as part of the substantial completion certificate.

A punch list does not address code issues. The inspectors having jurisdiction will be responsible for code compliance and issuing a U&O or temporary occupancy permit until all code violations have been corrected. It is important to note that some code violations are not life safety issues. For instance, if you have some landscaping that has not been established, a temporary U&O may be granted by the jurisdiction having authority. Make sure your design firm is familiar with the code officials in your area, because during RFP review it is crucial to know what the local code officials expect regarding code compliance.

8

Project Closeout

Project closing, while a fairly routine process, can require a substantial amount of time on the part of the project manager. It may take as long as one year before a project's final report and archiving is completed. The following checklist includes, but is not limited to, items that may need reviewed and recorded in an after-action report that will help the ongoing transition of a project from completion to operation and maintenance.

• Make sure users are satisfied with the end product and obtain final approval documents (signed by user agency)
• Conduct and record a lessons-learned meeting with all the stakeholders
• Record comparisons of the original project charter and the actual outcomes regarding time, quality, and costs, along with comparison of methods, techniques, and tools used during the project, and record their effectiveness
• Disband resources
• Archive project records
• Develop user feedback questionnaires as a technique for gathering comments from key staff, i.e., maintenance, facility management staff, and any other operational users of the end product

AS-BUILT DRAWINGS

As part of the construction contract, the contractor is required to provide the owner as-built drawings/record drawings as outlined in the project manual (see appendix D, Section 01781). As-built drawings represent a deviation from intended installations of construction items compared to their actual physical location after installation. As a project proceeds through the construction process, changes can arise due to RFI requests, change orders, unforeseen site conditions, value engineering, and so on. In order to capture these field changes, as-built drawings are developed after construction has been completely finished, and include punch list items.

Working together, the construction inspector and contractor will record field changes and develop a combined set of as-built drawings that will later be drafted into some type of electronic format, such as CADD. In an effort to keep track of all the field changes, monthly as-built submissions should be made to the design firm for review and later record drawing production when combining field changes made by all subcontractors during construction. When reviewing these as-built drawings, the design firm may determine that the original drawings and shop drawings are not detailed enough to show the actual installation; in this case, new drawings may be required via a change order (see appendix G).

FINAL ACCEPTANCE

When the contractor considers the work to be completed, they will submit a certification letter to the construction inspector, PM, and design firm indicating that final completion requirements have been met. The notice for a certificate of final completion may include the completion of the following checklist items in writing as part of the acceptance criteria.

- Contractor's review of the contract documents has been completed.
- The contractors verified that they have inspected the work.
- Work deficiencies listed on the punch list included in the certificate of substantial completion have been corrected. A copy of the punch list with the initials of the construction inspector, PM, facility users, and design firm is included.
- The contractor has verified equipment has been tested, adjusted, balanced, and is operational.
- The operation of systems has been demonstrated to maintenance personnel.
- As-built drawings and project record documents have been approved and submitted to the PM.

After submission of the final completion certificate, the contractor can set up a final inspection with the construction inspector. With a date established for final completion, the construction inspector will perform a final completion inspection and a re-inspection if required. It is important for the contractor to make sure that all the items are completed beforehand, because their final payment will be directly related to final acceptance. If it is evident that items are still outstanding, the contractor will need to continue insurance coverage until final acceptance is obtained.

Once final acceptance is approved, the contractor will then submit any and all closeout submittals that will include evidence of compliance with authorities having jurisdiction, a certificate of occupancy or a U&O, certificates for any conveying systems, operation and maintenance manuals, warranties and bonds, evidence of release of liens, and consent of surety bond to final payment.

AFTER-ACTION REPORT

After the contractor has demobilized and the construction inspector has completed the required work, PMs will develop a document, also referred to as a post-implementation evaluation report (PIER) document that summarizes how the project performed during construction from start to finish. This document will later be reviewed to perform continuous improvements to the project management process using the philosophies that make up a quasi-Kaizen approach. Kaizen is a practice that focuses upon continuous improvement of processes in many industries including management. It helps to measure current requirements against realistic conditions, increase productivity, and improve current operational standards. Figure 8.1 is an example of an after-action report based on our sample project shown in figure 1.1.

LESSONS LEARNED

As part of an after-action report, mistakes made during design and construction are listed in a risk register, also known as a risk log, so that they can be avoided on future projects (see appendix J). As part of an organization's program for continued improvement, weekly or bi-weekly meetings within the PMO need to be scheduled so that mistakes can be cataloged and entered into a collection of lessons learned documents that can be viewed by performing a keyword search in a lessons learned database. This will allow other PMs who may have a similar issues access to the same work-around technique to accomplish a given task. It will also identify areas of a project that will help keep the triple constraints better balanced.

Based on figure 1.1 we would develop a final after-action report that includes a lessons learned section, listed in figure 8.1.

(Insert Division name)

(Insert Department name)

OFFICE OF PROJECT MANAGEMENT

(Insert address)

TO: Director, Division of Public Works

THROUGH: Department Head, Program Development & Management

THROUGH: Engineering Manager, Office of Project Management

FROM: Kevin Vida, Project Manager, Office of Project Management

DATE: January 27, 2008

Re: Final Report- Anytown Fire Company #1 Fire Station

CIP Project # (Enter number)

Purpose of This Report

OPM staff created this report in order to provide relevant information about project scope, account balances, change orders, and lessons learned during the project. Use of the report during design and construction of future projects will increase our success in terms of budget variances, schedule execution, and user satisfaction.

Project Scope of Work

The Anytown Fire Company #1 Fire Station project was designed to house a combination of volunteer and paid personnel that provide both fire and rescue operations. The station was designed to house an Ambulance equipped for basic life support, two pumpers, a quick response vehicle, and a tanker. A ladder truck could be added if needed. The Facility includes four double-stacked equipment bays, administration areas, support spaces such as living quarters and equipment support areas.

Office/support spaces:	5,537 SF
Apparatus Bay:	5,230 SF
Total project SF:	10,767 SF
Notice to Proceed:	10/02/2006
Original Contract Completion Date:	05/30/2007
Revised Contract Completion Date:	09/19/2007
Substantial Completion Established:	08/30/2007

Figure 8.1.1

Final Acceptance:	08/30/2008
Construction Funds:	**$2,578,406.50**
	(Contract amount awarded)

Cost of A/E Contract: A/E PO # (insert PO number)

A/E original contract & fees:	$250,000.00
Original P.O. Amount to A/E:	$184,000.00
Total Change Order Amount:	$60,407.50
Total PO + CO Amount:	$244,407.50
Total Invoiced Amount:	$239,615.71
Remaining account Balance:	$10,384.29

Project Management, Inspection, Design, Construction, and Site Costs:

The actual costs for these accounts are shown on the following pages. These figures were compiled from the Detailed Budget Transaction Report.

Project Management Costs (Insert Project & Account number):

Original Budget Amount	$70,500.00
Amended Budget Amount	$83,000.00
Expended Amount	$78,500.00
Permit fees	$5,300.00
Nextel	$800.00
DPW Salary / Fringe Distribution	$69,000.00
Unknown / Miscellaneous	$900.00
Printing / Postage/in-house copies	$2,500.00
Budget Balance Remaining	$4,500.00

Inspection Costs (Insert Project & Account number):

Original Budget Amount	$200,500.00
Amended Budget Amount	$210,500.00
Expended Amount	$207,700.00
Nextel	$2,300.00
Inspections	$6,800.00
Vehicle Recovery	$1,100.00
DPW Salary / Fringe Distribution	$187,300.00
Inspection – IDQ	$10,200.00
Budget Balance Remaining	$2,800.00

A /E total fees (Insert Project & Account number):

Figure 8.1.2

Original Budget Amount	$250,000.00
Amended Budget Amount	$273,000.00
Expended Amount	$269,250.00
A/E original contract amount	$180,000.00
A/E Change Orders #1	$60,500.00
A/E Change Orders#2 thru 5	$20,500.00
Printing & Postage	$5,000.00
Title work	$650.00
Permit fees	$2,600.00
Budget Balance Remaining	$3,750.00

Project Management costs were estimated at 2.60% .The actual cost was 2.79%. The cost overrun can be attributed to permit fees. There were several Project Managers assigned to this project. The final Project Manager was Kevin Vida. Total costs of permits were $57,887.38. Inspection costs were estimated at 7.4%. Actual cost was 7.56% of the construction budget. The Architectural costs were estimated at 9.00% of the construction budget. The actual cost was 10.00%. The overage in A/E fees can be attributed to the lag in the project schedule due to the Organization impounding the construction funds for a year thus requiring a re-design change order.

Change Order Summary

The following tables highlight the change orders processed for the project.

Change Order description	QTY	Total Amount	% of Total bid
User requested	5	-$805.45	-0.03%
Unforeseen conditions	15	($30,781.24)	1.19%
Error and Omission	5	($38,781.24)	1.49%
Credit change order	1	-$27,532.50	-1.07%
Change order TOTALS	26	BID Total $2,578,405.50	% Total 1.04%

Change orders totaled 1.04% of the construction budget, the majority in regards to both quantity and dollar amount is considered an acceptable rate within the construction industry.

Remaining Account Balances

The remaining account balances are shown below. The chart reflects account balances as shown in the budget as of January 21, 2008

Figure 8.1.3

Organization Budget Status (January 21, 2008)

	Budgeted Amount	Encumbered Amount	Expended Amount	Expenditure to Date	Remaining Balance
A/E Design	$250,000	$273,000	$269,250.	$269,250	$3,750
Site	$49,600	$49,600	$49,600	$49,600	$0
Project Management	$70,500	$83,000	$78,500	$78,500	$4,500
Inspection	$200,500	$210,500	$207,700	$207,700	$2,800
Construction	$2,707,235	$2,578,406	$2,578,406	$2,578,406	$128,829
Equipment	$78,024	$75,791	$75,791	$75,791	$2,233
Total	$3,355,859	$3,270,297	$3,259,247	$3,259,247	$140,112

Lessons Learned

1. Use the following roof anchors (SUPER Z-PURLIN ANCHOR)
2. Wall cabinets need to be at least 15" deep.
3. Some stations may require opticon system coordination with SHA.
4. A fireproof cabinet purchased under the furniture account is required in the bay before life safety approval.
5. An add alternate is needed so that a price can be obtained for a Magna-Grip System.
6. Use a 12 AWG for cord reels. Include a quick release plug or breakaway plug at the cord reel end, so not to tear out from drive offs.
7. Make sure HVAC shut-down is included in FA.
8. Make the extractor space bigger and base design on 60 LB. Uni-Mac.
9. Use the Trench drain dimensions on the Arch. plans. (12" x 12" x 36")
10. Makeup air in storage area to have smoke dampers that are tied into the FA panel.
11. Grit separator vents need to run to the building. Also verify if the grit separator is in the sidewalk verify opening sizes to accommodate equipment hatch openings
12. Use jack shaft motors on doors.
13. Install a double vertical backflow preventer on the truck fills.
14. Provide door sweeps and thresholds for the doors entering the bay from the office space.
15. Make the turn-out gear room larger.
16. Vent Turn-out gear room to the outside (Min. 180 CFM).
17. Use a range hood that has ansul installed.
18. Use a Galaxy Model 508i (eight) x 2 for basis of designing rough-in only. IIT will have a separate contract to install the wire and components.
20. IITs supplier will provide electric strikes for panic doors.
21. Best hardware only on all projects.
22. Make sure counter tops do not interfere with drawers.
23. Make sure all color samples are approved during design.
24. Parking areas should be concrete to avoid pavement failures.
25. Fitness area will need higher ceilings.
26. A tower and mezzanine may be cost effective when training staff on a daily basis.
27. Verify the style of backflow preventer to meet the plumbing code at the main water line into the building.

Figure 8.1.4

28.   Provide sufficient depth for the water line entering the building to be below the footing.
29.   Verify that all condensate drains exiting the building are independent of the sanitary waste drains per plumbing code.
30.   Washer/extractor; provide proper floor thickness with sufficient trench drain.
31.   Larger mail boxes with slotted faces and individual locks on doors.
32.   Provide better designed hand-railings.
33.   Verify that the structural steel will do 2 things; 1) Support components and any suggested methods of attachment to the steel. 2) Verify the wind column design will accommodate the roll-up doors and we don't have to shift anything.
34.   Verify that the climate control devices will fit in the data room/closet with IIT networking components.
35.   Coordinate or identify open spaces on walls to mount hose racks and fire equipment in the apparatus bay.
36.   Provide the color coded emergency response lighting in the living areas. (Blue & Red)
37.   Have users verify keying meeting minutes and attend all pre-install meetings.
38.   If a mezzanine level is built in the building and an equipment access door is installed, provide railing at the door to meet building code.
39.   During the first year of operation, specify who is to maintain Fire Alarm monitoring the owner or the contractor, and if the contractor who does the user want to use?
40.   Make sure that all fire lane stripping is shown on plans.
41.   Will the users want to install their logo on the floor?
42.   Have Maintenance verify the AIR handling system meets their approval before construction to avoid additional duct after construction. Verify, if changed, the unit will fit in the space allotted.
43.   Appliances – To be Commercial Grade.
44.   Dishwasher to be the correct style.
45.   Counter Tops should not have large overhangs over drawers.
46.   Garage Door Openers to work both ways. Should be able to open and close doors with remote.
47.   Night Lights in Bunk Room should be enough to light the isle when alerted in place of ceiling lights.
48.   Lights in Gear Room to be incandescent.
49.   The lines in the engine room floors to be the correct width. The dimensions should have been inside diameter not outside diameter.
50.   The Alert System needs to be updated.
51.   Letters on the building and sign need more contrast.
53.   Street Numbers are required on both the building and site sign.
54.   Electric should be run to a single room instead of down every wall in the engine bay.
56.   Fitness Room, in addition to the higher ceilings, the proper flooring should be used in place of standard carpet.
57.   Engine bay doors should be 14' wide and 14' tall.
58.   Pantry area should be larger and securable for each shift.
59.   Number of lockers in locker rooms should equal number of personnel assigned to the station.
60.   Building needs to be sized appropriately and not sized for the current needs.
61.   Dumpster screen shall be a masonry construction type, not wood.

Figure 8.1.5

62. The work area, in the watch office, should be provided by the contractor and not as part of the furniture. Problems were encountered with counter tops fitting properly. (Built in work areas)

Outstanding Issues

1. We had some HVAC temperature control problems in the bunkroom.

Items to Monitor

1. Pavement humps in drive isle. It might be due to water break.

Figure 8.1.6

PROJECT ARCHIVING

Before submitting files to an archive, the PM will need to have developed a system of files in which the project documents reside. Since almost all PMs are converting from paper files to electronic file storage, the following is an example of electronic folders identifying active project documents. As a project proceeds, documentation is stored under the following active electronic folders for archiving at a later date:

Anytown Fire Company #1 Fire Station
1. Correspondence
   a. Design
      - Consultant correspondence
      - Transmittals
      - e-mails
   b. Construction
      - Warranties
      - Close out
      - Punch out
2. Design phases
   a. Programming
      - Feasibility study
      - Space study
   b. 15% schematic design
      - 15% review comments
   c. 35% design documents
      - 35% review comments
      - 35% cost estimate

  d. 50% construction documents
   • 50% review comments
   • 50% cost estimate
  e. 95% construction documents
   • 95% comments
   • 95% cost estimate
  f. 100% final documents
   • Final review
   • Signatures on bid sets
   • Front end document development
3. Bid Phase
  a. Advertisement
  b. Pre-bid
  c. Bid opening
4. Meeting minutes
  a. Design
  b. Construction
5. Organizational briefs
6. Contract documents
  a. Proof of insurance design firm and contractors
  b. Design firm RFP and award
  c. Design firm contract
  d. Construction bid and award
  e. Construction contract
7. Contract deviations
  a. Design RFIs
  b. Design PCOs
  c. Design change orders
  d. Construction RFIs
  e. Construction PCOs
  f. Construction change orders
8. Reports
  a. Geotechnical
  b. Hazmat—environmental
  c. Space studies
  d. Feasibility studies
  e. Archeological
9. Financial
  a. General budget information
  b. Budget requests
  c. Grants

10. Invoices
    a. Design
    b. Construction
11. Permits
    a. Site plan
    b. Improvement plans
    c. Environmental
    d. Building
    e. Electrical power
    f. Gas company
    g. Data/phone
    h. Fire marshal
    i. Planning and zoning
    j. Water/sewer fees
12. Easements
    a. ALTA Survey
    b. Right-of-way (ROW) agreements
13. Schedules
    a. Design
    b. Construction
14. Construction submittals
    a. Submittal log
    b. Shop drawings/cut sheets submittals
    c. As-builts
15. Special issues
16. Drawings and specifications
    a. Exiting drawings
    b. User specifications
    c. User SOPs
    d. User OPR

Upon gathering and verifying all project documentation, the PM will start the archiving process so that historic data can be introduced to an electronic depository. This allows other staff easy access and use as a tool for identifying, mitigating, and improving a similar project. Archived documents may include the following:

• Project charter: Known as the CIP plan describing the individual project needs. The PM needs to include the project description and plan, and documents showing project buy-in from the stakeholders.
• Project budget: Comparisons of assigned and actual project costs.

- Work breakdown structure (WBS): Review the work activities and identify any improvements made during the project.
- Contracts: Includes all contract documents signed by all stakeholders and contractors.
- Communication plan: Includes staff and vendor information so future inquiries can be performed.
- Construction meeting minutes: Used to document actual construction progress, it can be used to verify when construction activities took place and grade construction performance.
- Change orders: Details of all change orders accumulated during the project, describing why the change was needed, the cost, tools and techniques used to successfully process the change with little or no effect to time or quality, and in some cases, price.
- Stakeholder and user sign-off: The stakeholders and users will sign a form indicating the work has been performed per the project plan and specifications.
- Status reports: This is a final document generated based on project progress during design and construction, identifying any risks encountered, techniques used to mitigate them or workarounds that may have been used, along with their effectiveness.
- Lessons learned: This document is filed so that another PM can access a database and by keyword searching, find workarounds that may have worked during your project and apply those tools, methods, or techniques to their ongoing project.
- Checklists: Developed from documents such as those listed for design reviews and final punch lists, these provide a road map of what to review or provide.
- Technical Documents: These would be any drawings, sketches, as-builts, specifications, and/or project manuals used during the project. It also needs to include approved submittals, operation and maintenance manuals, and warranty information.

List of Online Appendixes

The following appendixes can be found at https://rowman.com/ISBN/
9781605907888

Appendix A   Request for Statements of Qualifications (SOQ)
Appendix B   Request for Proposal (RFP)
Appendix C   Indefinite Quantity Contract (IDQ) for A/E Services
Appendix D   Front End Specifications
Appendix E   Suggested Construction Contract (EJCDC C-520) and Contract Checklist (EJCDC C050)
Appendix F   Contractor's Application for Payment (EJCDC C-620)
Appendix G   Change Order (EJCDC C-941)
Appendix H   Work Change Directive (EJCDC C-940)
Appendix I   Substantial Completion Form (EJCDC C-625)
Appendix J   Lessons Learned Form
Appendix K   Cost Estimate Classification System
Appendix L   Qualifications Based Selection Workbook
Appendix M   As-builts: Problems and Proposed Solutions

Notes and Sources

NOTES

1. Project Management Institute (PMI), *A Guide to the Project Management Body of Knowledge* (*PMBOK Guide*), third edition, 5. Newtown Square, PA: Project Management Institute, 2004.

2. PMI, *PMBOK Guide*, 8.

3. PMI, *PMBOK Guide*, 378.

4. PMI, *PMBOK Guide*, 38.

5. Kim Heldman, *Project Management Professional Study Guide*, second edition, 87. Alameda, CA: SYBEX Inc., 2002.

6. Massachusetts Department of Revenue, *Developing a Capital Improvements Program*, 3. Boston: Massachusetts Department of Revenue, 1997.

7. Massachusetts Department of Revenue, *Developing a Capital Improvements Program*, 8.

8. Nick Hanley and Clive L. Spash, *Cost-Benefit Analysis and the Environment*, 11. Cheltenham, UK: Edward Elgar Publishing, 1993.

9. PMI, *PMBOK Guide*, 28.

10. PMI, *PMBOK Guide*, 358.

11. Heldman, *Project Management Professional Study Guide*, 290.

12. PMI, *PMBOK Guide*, 256–57, 361, 378.

13. PMI, *PMBOK Guide*, 368.

14. PMI, *PMBOK Guide*, 356–57, 378.

15. PMI, *PMBOK Guide*, 145.

16. Andy Crowe, *The PMP Exam: How to Pass on Your First Try*, 143. Kennesaw, GA: Velociteach Press, 2005.

17. Michigan QBS Coalition, Detailed Workbook for Qualifications-based Selection, 2004, 4. http://www.qbs-mi.org/pdf/2004_QBS_workbook.pdf.

18. Material reproduced with permission of the University of Michigan-Architecture, Engineering, and Construction (UM-AEC), 326 East Hoover, Ann Arbor, MI

48109-1002. For more information, permissions, suggestions, or questions regarding these and other documents, visit http://www.umaec.umich.edu or contact aexwebsite@umich.edu.

19. American Society of Heating, Refrigeration, and Air-conditioning Engineers (ASHRAE) Standards Committee, *ASHRAE Guideline: The Commissioning Process*, 6. Atlanta, GA: ASHRAE, Inc., 2005. http://unmsrmc.org/rfp/wp-content/uploads/2011/02/ASHRAE-Guideline-0-The-Commissioning-Process.pdf.

20. Material reproduced with permission of the University of Michigan-Architecture, Engineering, and Construction (UM-AEC), 326 East Hoover, Ann Arbor, MI 48109-1002. For more information, permissions, suggestions, or questions regarding these and other documents, visit http://www.umaec.umich.edu or contact aexwebsite@umich.edu.

21. Material reproduced with permission of Associated Builders and Contractors, Virginia Chapter General Contractor's Council, "Constructability Checklist." http://ps.businesssocialinc.com/media/uploads/abcva/constructability%20checklist.pdf.

SOURCES

http://www.usgbc.org/DisplayPage.aspx?CMSPageID=2465

http://www.agecon.purdue.edu/staff/shively/COURSES/AGEC406/reviews/bca.htm

http://www.aurorawdc.com/dlj_cics_npv_analysis.pdf

http://www.dramatispersonae.org/DesignEconomics/cpmNotes(ToddHeadon).pdf

http://www.tpub.com/content/construction/14043/css/14043_263.htm

https://www.acquisition.gov/far/html/Subpart%2015_4.html

https://www.acquisition.gov/far/current/html/Subpart%2016_3.html

http://www.qbs-mi.org/pdf/WhyValuebyMCooper.pdf

http://webcache.googleusercontent.com/search?q=cache:FBmKadN4ipEJ:hawaii.gov/formscentral/internal/information-and-communication-services-division/instructions/icsd256i.doc/at_download/file+icsd+contractors&cd=4&hl=en&ct=clnk&gl=us&client=firefox-a

http://factory.engr.stthomas.edu/monson/Files/EarnedValueTechniques.pdf

www.aurorawdc.com/dlj_cics_npv_analysis.pdf

http://www.qbs-mi.org/pdf/EngineeringInc-4-2010.pdf

http://www.qbs-mi.org/pdf/2004_QBS_workbook.pdf

http://www.nsf.gov/about/contracting/rfqs/support_ant/docs/facility_manuals/palmer_mcm_and_southpole/costestimatingsystemaace-208a.pdf

http://cmaanet.org/files/as-built.pdf

http://www.anvari.net/Risk%20Analysis/17r-97.pdf

http://www.ima.kth.se/utb/mj2694/pdf/CBA.pdf

Glossary and General Terms

68-95-99.7 rule: States that for a normal distribution, nearly all values lie within three standard deviations of the mean. About 68.26% of the values lie within one standard deviation of the mean; 95.44% of the values lie within two standard deviations, and 99.73% of the values lie within three standard deviations of the mean.

Accept: The act of formally receiving or acknowledging something and regarding it as being true, sound, suitable, or complete.

Acceptance: See *accept.*

Acceptance criteria: Those criteria, including performance requirements and essential conditions, which must be met before project deliverables are accepted.

Activity: A component of work performed during the course of a project. See also *schedule activity.*

Activity attributes: Multiple attributes associated with each schedule activity that can be included within the activity list. Activity attributes include activity codes, predecessor activities, successor activities, logical relationships, leads and lags, resource requirements, imposed dates, constraints, and assumptions.

Activity code: One or more numerical or text values that identify characteristics of work or in some way categorize the schedule activity that allows filtering and ordering of activities within reports.

Activity description (AD): A short phrase or label for each schedule activity used in conjunction with an activity identifier to differentiate that project's schedule activity from other schedule activities. The activity description normally describes the scope of work of the schedule activity.

Activity duration: The time in calendar units between the start and finish of a schedule activity, i.e., task.

Activity duration estimating: The process of estimating the number of work periods that will be needed to complete individual schedule activities.

Activity identifier: A short unique numeric or text identification assigned to each schedule activity to differentiate that project activity from other activities. Typically unique for any one project schedule network diagram.

Activity list: A document tabulation of schedule activities that shows the activity description, activity identifier, and a sufficiently detailed scope of work description so that project team members understand what work is to be performed.

Activity on arrow (AOA): See *arrow diagramming method.*

Activity on node (AON): See *precedence diagramming method.*

Activity resource estimating: The process of estimating the types and quantities of resources required to perform each schedule activity.

Activity sequencing: The process of identifying and documenting dependencies among schedule activities.

Actual cost (AC): Total costs actually incurred and recorded in accomplishing work performed for a schedule activity, i.e., task, or work breakdown structure component. Actual cost can sometimes be direct labor hours alone, direct costs alone, or all costs including indirect costs. Also referred to as the actual cost of work performed (ACWP). See also *earned value technique.*

Actual cost of work performed (ACWP): *See actual cost.*

Addenda: Used during the bidding process, it is a document developed to provide responses to RFIs from contractors and overrides and previously described directions in the original contract documents.

Adequate public facilities ordinance (APFO): A prerequisite to having a site plan approved by the jurisdiction having authority. It is an ordinance that requires developers to install roads, water and sewer, stormwater management facilities, or even schools before building any other structures on a proposed site.

ALTA Survey (American Land Title Association Survey): Produced for commercial properties using a set of minimum standards developed by ALTA and the American Congress on Surveying and Mapping (ACSM) for preparing a boundary survey, it shows all elements that impact the land, such as improvements, easements, and right-of-ways.

Analogous estimate: An estimating technique that uses the values of parameters, such as scope, cost, budget, and duration or measures of scale such as size, weight, and complexity, from a previous similar activity as the basis for estimating the same parameter or measure for a future activity. It is frequently used to estimate a parameter when there is a limited amount of detailed information about the project, such as during the schematic design. Analogous estimating is a form of expert judgment. Analogous estimating is most reliable when the previous activities are similar in fact and not just in appearance, and the project team members preparing the estimates have the needed expertise.

Application area: A category of projects that have common components significant in such projects, but are not needed or present in all projects. Application areas are usually defined in terms of either the product (i.e., by similar technologies or production methods) or the type of customer (i.e., internal versus external, government versus commercial) or industry sector (i.e., utilities, automotive, aerospace, information technologies). Application areas can overlap.

Approved request change: A change request that has been processed through the integrated change control process and approved. Contrast with requested change.

Arrow diagramming method: A schedule network diagramming technique in which schedule activities, i.e., tasks, are represented by arrows. The tail of the arrow represents the start and the head represents the finish of the task. (The length of the arrow does not represent the expected duration of the task.) Tasks are connected at points called nodes (usually drawn as small circles) to illustrate the sequence in which the tasks are expected to be performed. See also *precedence diagramming method.*

Backward pass: The calculation of late finish dates and late start dates for the uncompleted portions of all tasks, determined by working backwards through the schedule network logic from the project's end date. The end date may be calculated in a forward pass or set by the user. See also *schedule network analysis.*

Balancing change order: Used to encumber unused construction or design funds from their executed purchase order.

Bar charts: Also called Gannt charts, these show the start and finish dates of project tasks, and show the dependencies between work breakdown structure activities.

Baseline: The approved time phased plan (for a project, a work breakdown structure component, a work package, or a schedule activity), plus or minus approved project scope, cost, schedule, and technical changes. Generally refers to the current baseline, but may refer to the original or some other baseline. Usually used with a modifier (e.g., cost baseline, schedule baseline, performance measurement baseline, technical baseline). Also see *performance measurement baseline.*

Basic ordering agreements (BOAs)/indefinite delivery contract: This is a contract that contains information regarding future contacts within a defined time period. Future contracts will include a Statement of Work. They are usually used when negotiating a fixed-price or cost-reimbursement contract.

Benchmarking: The process of comparing performance and best practices to better balance the triple constraint by doing things better, faster, and more cost effectively. This then allows organizations to develop plans on how to make continuous improvements.

Bid documents: Instructions, such as construction documents or project manuals (i.e., specifications) used to obtain a fair price for a product or service.

Bid phase services: Designated design firm service used during the bidding process to produce responses to RFIs and provide a recommendation for award.

Board of county commissioners (BOCC): Similar to a board of directors, it is the body of county governments that act on behalf of their constituency and is the final authority for approving or rejecting project requests and funds.

Boilerplate documents: Previously developed documents used on past projects that allow a project manager to tailor them to fit their particular project.

Bottom-up estimating method: A method of estimating a component of work. The work is decomposed into more detail. An estimate of what is needed to meet the requirements of each of the lower, more detailed pieces of work is prepared, and these estimates are then aggregated into a total quantity for the component of work. The accuracy of bottom-up estimating is driven by the size and complexity of the work identified at the lower levels. Generally smaller work scopes increase the accuracy of the estimates.

Brainstorming: A general data gathering and creativity technique that can be used to identify risks, ideas, or solutions to issues by using a group of team members or subject-matter experts. Typically, a brainstorming session is structured so that each participant's ideas are recorded for later analysis.

Brick-and-mortar money: Describes funds specifically allocated for construction and cannot be used as operating funds.

Budget amendment: Used when a project account needs unencumbered funds to allow the account to maintain a positive balance.

Budgeted cost of work performed (BCWP): See *earned value.*

Budgeted cost of work scheduled (BCWS): See *planned value.*

Building inspector: Jurisdictional representative having authority to issue use and occupancy permits, once facilities meet all building code requirements per jurisdiction code requirements.

Building permits office: Functioning as part of the local government having jurisdictional authority in code matters, this office is used for applying and paying fees for review of construction documents, issuing of permits, and approving use and occupancy permits.

Capital budget: A document that provides a summary of all the expected projects to be budgeted for the next fiscal year and a potential outlook for project funding in the next year.

Capital program: The financing and implementation plan for a government organization's construction and renovation projects to organization-owned facilities and infrastructure over a six-fiscal-year (FY) period.

Change order: A tool used to add or delete work on an ongoing project. It requires organization approval before modifying the original contract.

Change request: Requests to expand or reduce the project scope, modify policies, processes, plans, or procedures, modify costs or budgets, or revise schedules. Request for a change can be direct or indirect, externally or internally initiated, and legally or contractually mandated to optional. Only formally documented requested changes are processed and only approved change requests are implemented.

Construction administration services: Design firms provide these services during project construction to review submittals, answer RFIs, recommend approval of pay requisitions, and provide inspection of the contractor's work to verify that the work is being installed per the specifications.

Construction change directive: Not a popular item in the construction industry, and used only as a last resort, this is a document that, per the construction contract, requires the contractor to act immediately on an item that is not clearly determined to be a change order and ends debate, forcing the contractor to install the item in question and allowing the work to be done without payment at that time, thus avoiding costly work stoppages.

Construction documents: Drawings and specifications used to bid a capital project. These provide direction to the potential bidders on how to and what to bid.

Construction inspector: This inspector monitors and administers work performed by the contractor in conjunction with the PM.

Construction management: An industry of its own, this department assigns and manages the construction once the general contractor's construction contracts are approved and executed.

Consultant selection committee (CSC): This committee approves the recommendation of proposed evaluators and the recommendation for awarding a design firm the contract through an request for proposal or qualifications-based selection process.

Control account (CA): A management control point where scope, budget (resource plans), actual cost, and schedule are integrated and compared to earned value for performance measurement. Control accounts are placed at selected management points (specific components at selected levels) of the work breakdown structures. Each control is associated with only one control account. Each control account is associated with a specific single organizational component in the organizational breakdown structure (OBS). Previously called a cost account.

Control chart: A graphic display of process data over time and against established control limits, and having a center line that assists in detecting a trend of plotted values toward either control limit.

Control limits: The area composed of three standard deviations on either side of the center line, or mean, of a normal distribution of data plotted on a control chart that reflects the expected variation in the data. See also *specifications limits.*

Cost-benefit analysis (CBA): Assigning a value to measure the worthiness of a project. CBA provides a mathematical process that justifies cost and need.

Cost estimate: Allows PMs a look-ahead with some certainty that the project is within the established project budget.

Cost management plan: A plan that is the output achieved by performing a cost estimate.

Cost performance index (CPI): A measure of cost efficiency on a project. It is the ratio of earned value (EV) to actual costs (AC). $CPI = EV \div AC$. A value equal to or greater than 1 indicates a favorable condition, and a value less than 1 indicates an unfavorable condition.

Cost-plus-fee (CPF): A type of cost-reimbursable contract where the buyer reimburses the seller for the seller's allowable costs for performing the contract work, and the seller also receives a fee calculated as an agreed-upon percentage of the costs. The fee varies with the actual cost.

Cost-plus-fixed fee (CPFF): A type of cost-reimbursable contract where the buyer reimburses the seller for the seller's allowable costs (allowable costs are defined by the contract) plus a fixed amount of profit (fee).

Cost-plus-incentive fee (CPIF): A type of cost-reimbursable contract where the buyer reimburses the seller for the seller's allowable costs (allowable costs are defined by the contract), and the seller earns its profit if it meets defined performance criteria.

Cost-plus-percentage of cost (CPPC): See *cost-plus-fee.*

Cost-reimbursement contracts: A type of contract involving payment (reimbursement) by the buyer to the seller for the seller's actual costs, plus a fee typically representing the seller's profit. Costs are usually classified as direct costs or indirect costs. Direct costs are costs incurred for the exclusive benefit of the project, such as salaries of full-time project staff. Indirect costs, also called overhead and general and administrative costs, are costs allocated to the project by the performing organization as a cost of doing business, such as salaries of management indirectly involved in the project and cost of electric utilities for the office. Indirect costs are usually calculated as a percentage of direct costs. Cost-reimbursable contracts often include incentive clauses where, if the seller meets or exceeds selected contract objectives, such as schedule targets or total cost, then the seller receives an incentive or bonus payment.

Cost variance (CV): A measure of cost performance on a project. It is the algebraic difference between earned value (EV) and actual cost (AC). CV = EV − AC. A positive value indicates a favorable condition and a negative value indicates an unfavorable condition.

Crashing: After the critical path has been identified, crashing is a specific type of project schedule compression technique performed by taking action to decrease the total project schedule duration after analyzing a number of alternatives to determine how to get the maximum schedule duration compression for the least additional cost. Typical approaches for crashing a schedule include reducing schedule activity durations and increasing the assignment of resources on tasks. See also *fast tracking*. After the critical path has been identified, it allows a projects schedule to shorten by adding more resources.

Critical claim method: This method plans a project based on resources to execute projects rather than CPM scheduling.

Critical path method (CPM): Known as the longest path through the entire project, it contains no float or slack time for tasks on the critical path. CPM is a schedule network analysis technique used to determine the amount of scheduling flexibility (the amount of float) on various logical project network paths in the project schedule network, and to determine the minimum total project duration. Early start and finish dates are calculated by means of a forward pass, using a specified start date. Late start and finish dates are calculated by means of a backward pass, starting from a specified completion date, which sometimes is the project early finish date determined during the forward pass calculation.

Customer: The person or organization that will use the project's product, service, or result. See also *stakeholder*.

Data date (DD): The date up to or through which the project's reporting system has provided actual status and accomplishments. In some reporting systems, the status information for the data date is included in the past and in other systems the status information is in the future. Also called as-of date and time-now date.

Date: A term representing the day, month, and year of a calendar, and in some instances, the time of day.

Definite quantity contract (DQC): This type of contract allows for purchase and installation of a defined quantity and specific supplies or services for a fixed period, with SOW performed upon task order execution.

Definitive estimate: A definitive estimate uses information based on data, specifications, or drawings, and is used for bidding purposes by an architect/engineer or contractor.

Deliverable: Any unique and verifiable product, result, or capability to perform a service that must be produced to complete a process, phase, or project. It is often used more narrowly in reference to an external deliverable, which is a deliverable that is subject to approval by the project sponsor or customer.

Delivery order contracts: This contract is for supplies and does not outline a specific quantity for services or supplies, but provides for executing task orders for the delivery of supplies during a specified time.

Delphi technique: An information-gathering technique used as a way to reach a consensus of experts on a subject. Experts on the subject participate in this technique anonymously. A facilitator uses a questionnaire to solicit ideas about the important project points related to the subject. The responses are summarized and are then recirculated to the experts for further comment. Consensus may be reached in a few rounds of this process. The Delphi technique helps reduce bias in the data and keeps any one person from having undue influence on the outcome.

Design-build contracts: This type of contract provides a total product. It is utilized in the architecture, engineering, and contruction industries. A design-build contract allows design and construction services to be provided as a combined service rather than using the "design-bid-build" method, making the service provider responsible for risks related to design and construction while reducing the owner's risks.

Design development documents (35% DDs): These documents allow the design firm to establish site plan elements and foundation plans.

Design documents: Includes all required directions for a contractor to construct the end product.

Design firm: Considered the subject matter expert, the design firm is the contracted entity that provides all design-related elements of a project.

Design permits: Reviewed and approved by the jurisdiction having authority, these permits are required before building permits can be reviewed and approved.

Design review: A management technique used for evaluating a proposed design to ensure that the design of the system or product meets the customer requirements, or to assure that the design will perform successfully, can be produced, and can be maintained.

Design team: Includes the A/E and all the subconsultants required to develop the contract drawings and provide recommendations and reviews, along with recommending approval of pay requisitions and responding to requests for information.

Early finish date (EF): Relative to the critical path method, the earliest possible point in time on which the uncompleted portions of a task (or the project) can finish, based on the schedule network logic, the data date, and any schedule constraints. Early finish dates can change as the project progresses and as changes are made to the project management plan.

Early start date (ES): In the critical path method, the earliest possible point in time on which the uncompleted portions of the schedule activity (or the project) can start, based on the schedule network logic, the data date, and any schedule constraints. Early start dates can change as the project progresses and as changes are made to the project management plan.

Earned value (EV): The value of work performed, expressed in terms of the approved budget assigned to that work for a schedule activity or work breakdown structure component. It is also referred to as the budgeted cost of work performed (BCWP).

Earned value technique (EVT): A specific technique for measuring the performance of work and used to establish the performance measurement baseline (PMB). It is also referred to as the earning rules and crediting method.

Economy of scale: A method used to create the advantage of lower costs through buying in bulk.

Environmental compliance section (EC): Approves and inspects the soil controls installed prior to construction. The section also inspects stormwater management facilities for compliance.

Error and/or omission change order: One of three types of change orders, this allows the owner to assess and assign penalties to the design firm for mistakes found during construction.

- Type I requires expending additional construction funds that would not have been needed had the design documents been accurate. The organization would pay for the items not covered under the specifications (betterment), and pursue recovery from the A/E for damages to the organization caused by A/E negligence.

- Type II requires expending additional construction funds that would not have been needed had the design documents been accurate. The A/E shall, without additional compensation, correct or revise any error or deficiencies in its designs, drawings, specifications, or other services. Cost of the betterment is to be borne by the organization. When appropriate, the organization will pursue recovery from the A/E of costs incurred by the organization related to additional staff time or outside consulting services to resolve the issue.

- Type III requires expending additional construction funds that would not have been needed had the design documents been accurate. The A/E shall, without additional compensation, correct or revise any error or deficiencies in its designs, drawings, specifications, or other services. Cost of the betterment is to be borne by the organization.

Estimate: A quantitative assessment of the likely amount or outcome. Usually applied to project costs, resources, effort, and duration, and is usually preceded by a modifier (i.e., preliminary, conceptual, feasibility, order-of-magnitude, definitive). It should always include some indication of accuracy (e.g., ±x percent).

Estimate at completion (EAC): The expected total cost of an activity, a group of activities, or of a project when the scope of the work has been completed. Most techniques for forecasting EAC include some adjustment of the original cost estimate based on project performance to date. Also shown as "estimated at completion." Often shown as EAC = actuals-to-date + actuals. See also earned value and estimate to complete.

Estimate to complete (ETC): The expected cost needed to complete all the remaining work for a schedule activity, work breakdown structure component, or the project. See also *earned value technique* and *estimate at completion.*

Event: Something that happens, an occurrence, and outcome.

Execute: Directing, managing, performing, and accomplishing the project work, providing the deliverables, and providing work performance information.

Expert judgment: Judgment provided based upon expertise in an application area, knowledge areas, discipline, industry, etc., as appropriate for the activity being performed. Such expertise may be provided by any group or person with specialized education, knowledge, skill, experience, or training, and is available from many sources, including other units within the performing organization; consultants; stakeholders, including customers; professional and technical associations; and industry groups.

Exterior insulation and finishing system (EIFS): A type of building exterior wall finishing system that provides an insulated and waterproof exterior surface.

Fast tracking: A specific project schedule compression technique that changes the network logic to overlap phases that would normally be done in sequence, such as the design phase and construction phase, or to perform schedule activities in parallel, which is a method of shortening the critical path by performing tasks concurrently and possibly adding resources.

Feasibility study: In relation to construction project management, this allows an organization to evaluate and identify risk via a risk management plan that will provide a go/no-go decision for purchasing and building on a potential project site.

Fee-in-lieu: A term describing monetary payment for products or services representing a cost equivalent to providing the same product or service.

Fee-not-to-exceed: A term related to predetermined funds that cannot be exceeded without a change order. Used mainly for reimbursable costs during design.

Field reports: Documented daily, these reports provide construction information, from the number of people working at the site to what jobs were performed, along with any weather conditions.

Finish date: A point in time associated with a schedule activity's completion, usually qualified by one of the following: actual, planned, estimated, scheduled, early, late, baseline, target, or current.

Finish-to-finish (FF): The logical relationship where completion of work of the successor activity cannot finish until the completion of work of the predecessor activity. See also *logical relationship.*

Finish-to-start (FS): The logical relationship where initiation of work of the successor activity depends upon the completion of work of the predecessor activity. See also *logical relationship.*

Firm-fixed-price contract (FFP): A type of fixed-price contract in which the buyer pays the seller a set amount (as defined by the contract), regardless of the seller's costs.

Fixed-price-incentive-fee contract (FPIF): A type of contract where the buyer pays the seller a set amount (as defined by the contract), and the seller can earn an additional amount if the seller meets defined performance criteria.

Fixed-price or lump-sum contract: A type of contract involving a fixed total price for a well-defined product. Fixed-price contracts may also include incentives for meeting or exceeding selected project objectives, such as schedule targets. The simplest form of a fixed price contract is a purchase order (PO).

Fixed-price redetermination contract: This contract allows for a firm fixed price for a predetermined amount of time and then is renegotiated approximately every 12 months thereafter. A fee-not-to-exceed clause may be used so that unforeseen conditions in performance can be minimized.

Fixed-price with economic price adjustment contract: This contract allows the flexibility to increase or decrease costs outlined in a previously approved contract based on current price indexes related to the service or supplies required.

Float: Also called slack, the amount of down time between the finish of one task and the start of the next task.

Forest resource ordinance (FRO): A permit requirement that requires a developer to not disturb or add a certain amount of trees as part of a reforestation effort. Some states may not require this.

Forward pass: The calculation of the early start and early finish dates for the uncompleted portions of all network activities. See also *schedule network analysis* and *backward pass.*

Free float (FF): The amount of time that a schedule activity can be delayed without delaying the early start of any immediately following scheduled activities. See also *total float.*

Front end documents: A set of instructions provided at the beginning of the project manual explaining what the contractor's and owner's responsibilities are.

Functional manager: Someone with management authority over an organizational unit within a functional organization; the manager of any group that actually makes a product or performs a service. Sometimes called a line manager.

Functional organization: A hierarchical organization where each employee has one clear superior, staff are grouped by areas of specialization, and are managed by a person with expertise in that area.

Future value (FV): This is the value of an asset or cash based on a future date, assuming a certain interest rate that is equal in value to a specified sum today.

Gannt chart: Also called a bar chart, it translates activity durations into a condensed snapshot as they relate to other activities throughout the project time line.

Gatekeeper: The person responsible for performing and monitoring specific activities as they relate to their area of expertise.

General contractor: A company bidding on contract documents to provide the means and methods to construct and make ready for use a final product.

General obligation bonds (GO): GO bonds allow government entities to obtain funds for maintaining or expanding necessary services for its constituency and is paid back using debt service payments, which is similar to mortgage payments.

Go/no-go decision: A term used to identify whether a project will proceed to the next phase or be closed.

Historical information: Documents and data in prior projects including project files, records, correspondence, closed contracts, and closed projects.

Improvement plans (IP): IPs need to be submitted to review agencies having jurisdiction regarding stormwater management requirements.

Indefinite quantity contract (IDQ): A method used by PMs to request a price for services that do not require a full RFP process. A task order is used to execute a PO and the work.

Initiating process: Those processes performed to authorize and define the scope of a new phase or project or that can result in the continuation of halted project work. A large number of the initiating processes are typically done outside the project's scope of control by the organization, program, or portfolio process, and those processes provide input to the project's initiating processes group.

Inspection: Examining or measuring to verify whether an activity, component, product result, or service conforms to specified requirements.

Integrated: Interrelated, interconnected, interlocked, or meshed components blended and unified into a functioning or unified whole.

Integrated change control: The process of reviewing all change requests, approving changes, and controlling changes to deliverables and organizational process assets.

Internal rate of return (IRR): Used for capital budgeting, this provides measurement of the profitability of a project.

Interviewers/evaluators: Recommended by the PM and approved by the CSC, they evaluate potential design firms through an RFP process.

Invitation for bid (IFB): Generally, this term is equivalent to request for proposal. However, in some application areas, it may have a narrower or more specific meaning.

Kaizen approach: Allows for continuous improvement of processes to make projects more cost effective.

Kick-off meeting: The first meeting held between the organization and its contracted design firm to establish lines of communication and indicates the official start of the design process.

Knowledge: Knowing something with the familiarity gained through experience, education, observation, or investigation, it is understanding a process, practice, or technique, or how to use a tool.

Lag: A modification of a logical relationship that directs a delay in the successor activity. For example, in a finish-to-start dependency with a 10-day lag, the successor activity cannot start until 10 days after the predecessor activity has vanished. See also *lead.*

Land acquisition coordinator: Provides all the services required for obtaining land or right-of-ways required for a project.

Late finish date (LF): In the critical path method, the latest possible point in time that a schedule activity may be completed based upon the schedule network logic, the project completion date, and any constraints assigned to the schedule activities without violating a schedule constraint or delaying the project completion date. The late finish dates are determined during the backward pass calculation of the project schedule network.

Late start date (LS): In the critical path method, the latest possible point in time that a schedule activity may begin based upon the schedule network logic, the project completion date, and any constraints assigned to the schedule activities without violating a schedule constraint or delaying the project completion date.

Latest revised estimate: See *estimate at completion.*

Lead: A modification of a logical relationship that allows an acceleration of the successor activity. For example, in a finish-to-start dependency with a 10-day lead, the successor activity can start 10 days before the predecessor activity has finished. See also *lag.* A negative lead is equivalent to a positive lag.

Lessons learned: The learning gained from the process of performing the project. Lessons learned may be identified at any point. Also considered a project record, it is a list of ways to improve project processes or avoid problems encountered during future projects.

Letter contract: A letter contract allows a supplier/vendor to begin work as soon as possible.

Leveling: See *resource leveling.*

Level of effort (LOE): Support-type activity (e.g., seller or customer liaison, project cost accounting, or project management), which does not produce definitive end products. It is generally characterized by a uniform rate of work performance over a period of time determined by the activities supported.

Life cycle: See *project life cycle.*

Logic: See *network logic.*

Logical relationship: A dependency between two project schedule activities, or between a project schedule activity and a schedule milestone. See also *precedence relationship.* The four possible types of logical relationships are finish-to-start, finish-to-finish, start-to-start, and start-to-finish.

Logic diagram: See *project schedule network diagram.*

Make-or-buy decision: A term used in project management that allows a company to determine if they should make a product in-house or subcontract it to a contractor.

Master schedule: A summary-level project schedule that identifies the major deliverables and work breakdown structure components and key schedule milestones. See also *milestone schedule.*

Matrix organization: Any organizational structure in which the project manager shares responsibility with the functional managers for assigning priorities and for directing the work of persons assigned to the project.

Means and methods of construction: Sequence of work that dictates how the contractor will provide and install project components to meet the requirement of the design. The contractor controls the means and methods of installation.

Metes and bounds: Surveying terms that describe the lengths, i.e., metes, between the bounds, i.e., property corners.

Milestone: An activity identified as having no time assigned to it but indicates a significant point or event in the project. See also *schedule milestone.*

Milestone schedule: A summary-level schedule that identifies the major schedule milestones. See also *master schedule.*

Monitor: To collect project performance data with respect to a plan, produce performance measures, and report and disseminate performance information.

Monitor and control project work: The process of monitoring and controlling the processes required to initiate, plan, execute, and close a project to meet the performance objectives defined in the project management plan and project scope statement.

Monitoring: See *monitor.*

Monitoring and controlling processes: Those processes performed to measure and monitor project execution so that corrective action can be taken when necessary to control the execution of the phase or project.

Monte Carlo analysis: A technique that computes, or iterates, the project cost or project schedule many times using input values selected at random from probability distributions of possible costs or durations to calculate a distribution of possible total project cost or completion dates.

National pollutant discharge elimination system (NPDES): As part of the Clean Water Act, 1972 amendments, NPDES is a regulatory system that enforces, through a local department of the environment, point sources of pollution such as industrial facilities, government facilities, and agricultural facilities/land using fertilizer.

Near-critical activity: A schedule activity that has low total float. The concept of near-critical is equally applicable to a schedule activity or schedule network path. The limit below which total float is considered near critical is subject to expert judgment and varies from project to project.

Net present value (NPV): Allows an organization to determine if a project is viable based on cash inflows and outflows.

Network: See *project schedule network diagram.*

Network analysis: See *schedule network analysis.*

Networking: Developing relationships with persons who may be able to assist in the achievement of objectives and responsibilities.

Network logic: The collection of schedule activity dependencies that makes up a project schedule network diagram.

Network path: Any continuous series of schedule activities connected with logical relationships in a project schedule network diagram.

Node: One of the defining points of a schedule network; a junction point joined to some or all of the other dependency lines. See also *arrow diagramming method* and *precedence diagramming method.*

Non-tidal wetlands permit: A regulatory notice and review indicating that your project is not destroying or disturbing any wetlands.

Notice of intent: A regulatory notice and review that informs the jurisdiction having authority that your project requires disturbing a certain amount of land (typically an acre or more).

Notice to proceed (NTP): A document that establishes the start time for design and/or construction of a project.

Objective: Something toward which work is to be directed, a strategic position to be attained, or a purpose to be achieved, a result to be obtained, a product to be produced, or a service to be performed.

Operations: An organizational function performing the ongoing execution of activities that produce the same product or provide a repetitive service. Examples are production operations, manufacturing operations, and accounting operations.

Opportunity: A condition or situation favorable to the project, a positive set of circumstances, a positive set of events, a risk that will have a positive impact on project objectives, or a possibility for positive changes. Contrast with *threat*.

Opportunity cost: The difference between choosing a more risky alternative for greater reward or staying with the original alternative that you know will provide no great reward.

Organization: A group of persons organized for some purpose or to perform some type of work within an enterprise.

Organization breakdown structure (OBS): A hierarchically organized depiction of the project organization, arranged to relate the work packages to the performing organizational units.

Organization chart: A method for depicting interrelationships among a group of persons working together toward a common objective.

Organizational process assets: Any or all process related assets, from any or all of the organizations involved in the project that are or can be used to influence the project's success. These process assets include formal and informal plans, policies, procedures, and guidelines. The process assets also include the organizations' knowledge bases such as lessons learned and historical information.

Original duration (OD): The activity duration originally assigned to a schedule activity and not updated as progress is reported on the activity, typically used for comparison with actual duration and remaining duration when reporting schedule progress.

Output: A product, result, or service generated by a process; may be an input to a successor process.

Owner's project requirements: A list of mechanical component functions that affect occupancy comfort and prioritize the functions so that the engineers can design systems accordingly.

Parametric estimating: An estimating technique that uses a statistical relationship between historical data and other variables (e.g., square footage in construction, lines of code in software development) to calculate an estimate for activity parameters, such as scope, cost, budget, and duration. This technique can produce higher levels of accuracy depending upon the sophistication and the underlying data built into the model. An example for the cost parameter is multiplying the planned quantity of work to be performed by the historical cost per unit to obtain the estimated cost.

Pareto chart: A histogram ordered by frequency of occurrence that shows how many results were generated by each identified cause.

Path convergence: The merging or joining of parallel schedule network paths into the same node in a project schedule network diagram. Path convergence is characterized by a schedule activity with more than one predecessor activity.

Path divergence: Extending or generating parallel schedule network paths from the same node in a project schedule network diagram. Path divergence is characterized by a schedule activity with more than one successor activity.

Payback period: The amount of time it takes to pay off a project debt.

Pay requisition: Generated from an invoice, it tracks all project payments to the design firm and the contractor and provides back-up justifying the invoice.

Percent complete (PC or PCT): An estimate, expressed as a percent, of the amount of work that has been completed on an activity or a work breakdown structure component.

Performance measurement baseline: An approved integrated scope-schedule-cost plan for the project work, against which project execution is compared to measure and manage performance. Technical and quality parameters may also be included.

Performance reporting: The process of collecting and distributing performance information. This includes status reporting, progress measurement, and forecasting.

Performance specification: A set of specific instruction related to how the organization requires a certain item to be provided, installed, and sequenced for operation.

Performing organization: The enterprise whose personnel are most directly involved in doing the work of the project.

Perform quality assurance (QA): The process of applying the planned, systematic quality activities (such as audits or peer reviews) to ensure that the project employs all processes needed to meet requirements.

Permit office: A centralized office for obtaining permits and scheduling inspections for projects.

Permits: Mechanisms used to inform the jurisdiction having authority that you are constructing something that requires inspections for code compliance.

Phase: See *project phase.*

Plan contracting: The process of documenting the products, services, and results requirements and identifying potential sellers.

Planned finish date (PF): See *scheduled finish date.*

Planned start date (PS): See *scheduled start date.*

Planned value (PV): The authorized budget assigned to the scheduled work to be accomplished for a schedule activity or work breakdown structure component. Also referred to as the budgeted cost of work scheduled (BCWS).

Planning and zoning: A department within the permit office that reviews and approves site plans, APFO, and FRO permits.

Planning commission: A group of appointed citizens that approves site plans according to the jurisdiction's code requirements related to site design.

Planning package: A work breakdown structure component below the control account with known work content but without detailed schedule activities. See also *control account.*

Plan purchases and acquisitions: The process of determining what to purchase or acquire, and determining when and how to do so.

Polychlorinated biphenyls (PCBs): Prior to 1979, were used widely as cooling fluid in transformers, electric motors, and hydraulic fluids.

Position description: An explanation of a project team member's roles and responsibilities.

Practice: A specific type of professional or management activity that contributes to the execution of a process and that may employ one or more techniques and tools.

Precedence diagramming method (PDM): Expresses activity sequencing using boxes (i.e., nodes) connected by arrows (AON) representing each required task and its time frame, packaged together to form an overall project task and time line.

Precedence network: A series of sequences that depend on a precedent and successor task that establish their relationship to the whole project.

Precedence relationship: The term used in the precedence diagramming method for a logical relationship. In current usage, however, precedence relationship, logical relationship, and dependency are widely used interchangeably, regardless of the diagramming method used.

Predecessor activity: The schedule activity that determines when the logical successor activity can begin or end.

Preliminary site plan: Prepared documents that establish site plan elements such as parking areas, stormwater management facilities, and building foundations, submitted to the permits office for planning commission approval.

Present value (PV): Based on a theory that cash today is worth more cash tomorrow, this allows an organization to take time out of the equation and determine how much a project is worth now. The more it is worth now, the better.

Preventative action: Documented direction to perform an activity that can reduce the probability of negative consequences associated with project risks.

Probability and impact matrix: A common way to determine whether a risk is considered low, moderate, or high by combining the two dimensions of a risk: its probability of occurrence, and its impact on objectives if it occurs.

Procedure: A series of steps followed in a regular definitive order to accomplish something.

Process: A set of interrelated actions and activities performed to achieve a specified set of products, results, or services.

Process group: See *project management process group.*

Procurement documents: Those documents utilized in bid and proposal activities, which include a buyer's invitation for bid, initiation for negotiations, request for information, request for quotation, request for proposal, and seller's responses.

Procurement management plan: The document that describes how procurement processes, from developing procurement documentation through contract closure, will be managed.

Procurement rules: Established by the purchasing division and approved by the organization, they are a collection of rules and guidelines followed when obtaining services or products.

Product: An artifact that is produced, is quantifiable, and can be either an end item in itself or a component item. Additional words for products are materials and goods. Contrast with result and service. See also *deliverable.*

Product life cycle: A collection of generally sequential, non-overlapping product phases whose name and number are determined by the manufacturing and control needs of the organization. The last product life cycle phase for a product is generally the product's deterioration and death. Generally, a project life cycle is contained within one or more product life cycles.

Product scope: The features and functions that characterize a product, service, or result.

Product scope description: The documented narrative description of the product scope.

Program: A group of related projects managed in a coordinated way to obtain benefits and control not available from managing them individually. Programs may include elements of related work outside of the scope of the discrete project in the program.

Program evaluation and review technique (PERT): Used to provide a breakdown of all the tasks required for a project and to assign the time needed to complete the task so that a total project timeline can be produced.

Program management: The centralized coordinated management of a program to achieve the program's strategic objectives and benefits.

Progressive elaboration: Continuously improving and detailing a plan as more detailed and specific information and more accurate estimates become available as the project progresses, and thereby producing more accurate and complete plans that result from the successive iterations of the planning process.

Progress reports: Prepared by PMs, a record document of project status regarding what work is completed and what work needs to be completed, along with documenting any issues that need or have been resolved.

Project: A temporary endeavor undertaken to create a unique product, service, or result.

Project calendar: A calendar of working days or shifts that establishes dates on which schedule activities are worked, and nonworking days that determine dates on which schedule activates are idle. Typically defines holidays, weekends and shift hours. See also *resource calendar*.

Project charter: A document describing the need for the project and authorizes the assignment of a project to a PM through the project management office. It also provides assurance from the organization's users, showing their commitment to a project.

Project closing: Performed as part of project completion, this requires obtaining and recording all project finalization documents formally identifying the end of a project.

Project initiation: Launching a process that can result in the authorization and scope definition of a new project.

Projectized organization: Any organizational structure in which the project manager has full authority to assign priorities, apply resources, and direct the work of persons assigned to the project.

Project life cycle: Represents all the tasks and activities performed from beginning to end of a project.

Project management (PM): The practice of identifying, assigning, and performing tasks to provide a unique service or product.

Project management body of knowledge: An inclusive term that describes the sum of knowledge within the profession of project management. As with other professions such as law, medicine, and accounting, the body of knowledge rests with the practitioners and academics that apply and advance it. The complete project management body of knowledge includes proven traditional practices that are widely applied and innovative practices that are emerging in the profession. The body of knowledge includes both published and unpublished materials. This body of knowledge is constantly evolving. PMI's *PMBOK® Guide* identifies that subset of the project management body of knowledge that is generally recognized as "good practice."

Project management office (PMO): The office responsible for performing all required project management tasks assigned by the organization. The PMO can be comprised of in-house staff or contracted from the private sector.

Project management plan: A formal, approved document that defines how the project is executed, monitored, and controlled. It may be summarized or detailed and may be composed of one or more subsidiary management plans and other planning documents.

Project management process group: A logical grouping of the project management processes described in the *PMBOK® Guide*. The project management process groups include initiation processes, planning processes, executing processes, monitoring and controlling processes, and closing processes. Collectively, these five groups are required for any project, have clear internal dependencies, and must be performed in the same sequence on each project, independent of the application area or the specifics of the applied project life cycle. Project management process groups are not project phases.

Project management professional (PMP®): A person certified as a PMP® by the Project Management Institute (PMI®).

Project management software: A class of computer software applications specifically designed to aid the project management team with planning, monitoring, and controlling the project, including cost estimating, scheduling, communications, collaboration, configuration management, document control, records management, and risk analysis.

Project management system: The aggregation of the processes, tools, techniques, methodologies, resources, and procedures to manage a project. The system is documented in the project management plan and its content will vary depending upon the application area, organizational influence, complexity of the project, and the availability of the existing systems. A project management system, which can be formal or informal, aids a project manager in effectively guiding a project to completion. A project management system is a set of processes and the related monitoring and control functions that are consolidated and combined into a functioning, unified whole.

Project management team: The members of the project team who are directly involved in project management activities. On some smaller projects, the project management team may include virtually all of the project team members.

Project manager (PM): Gatekeeper responsible for overall project success, the PM makes sure that the project is completed on time and within budget.

Project monitoring and controlling: Activities that allow project managers and construction inspectors to make sure the project is progressing both qualitatively and quantitatively.

Project organization chart: A document that graphically depicts the project team members and their interrelationships for a specific project.

Project phase: A collection of logically related project activities, usually culminating in the completion of a major deliverable. Project phases (also called phases) are mainly completed sequentially, but can overlap in some project situations. Phases can be subdivided into subphases and their components; this hierarchy, if the project or portions of the project are divided into phases, is contained in the work breakdown structure. A project phase is a component of a project live cycle. The project phase is not a project management process group.

Project planning: A process of developing project tasks, activities, and work packages that culminate into a total project plan.

Project process groups: The five process groups required for any projects that have clear dependencies and that are required to be performed in the same sequence on each project, independent of the application area or the specifics of the applied project life cycle. The process groups are initiating, planning, executing, monitoring and controlling, and closing.

Project schedule: The planned dates for performing schedule activities and the planned dates for meeting schedule milestones.

Project schedule network diagram: Any schematic display of the logical relationships among the project schedule activities. Always drawn from left to right to reflect project work chronology.

Project scope: The work that must be performed to deliver a product, service, or result with the specified features and functions.

Project scope management plan: The document that describes how the project scope will be defined, developed, and verified and how the work breakdown structure will be created and defined, and that provides guidance on how the project scope will be managed and controlled by the project management team. It is contained in or is a subsidiary plan of the project management plan. The project scope management plan can be informal and broadly framed, or formal and highly detailed, based on the needs of the project.

Project scope statement: The narrative description of the project scope, including major deliverables, project objectives, project assumptions, project constraints, and a statement of work, that provides a documented basis for making future project decisions and for confirming or developing a common understanding of project scope among the stakeholders.

Project team: All the project team members, including the project management team, the project manager and, for some projects, the project sponsor (i.e., the user).

Project team directory: A documented list of project team members, their project roles, and communication information.

Project team members: The persons who report either directly or indirectly to the project manager, and who are responsible for performing project work as a regular part of their assigned duties.

Proposed change orders (PCOs): PCOs and requests for tenders are used by a design firm or contractor to provide a fee proposal for work that was not part of the original contract.

Purchasing: A department comprised of purchasing and procurement managers that are the gate keepers of the RFP project.

Qualitative risk analysis: The process of prioritizing risks for subsequent further analysis or action by assessing and combining their probability of occurrence and impact.

Quality: The degree to which a set of inherent characteristics fulfills requirements.

Quality management plan: Plan describing how the project management team will implement the performing organization's quality policy. The quality management plan is a component or a subsidiary plan of the project management plan. The quality management plan may be formal or informal, highly detailed or broadly framed, based on the requirements of the project.

Quality planning: The process of identifying which quality standards are relevant to the project and determining how to satisfy them.

Quantitative risk analysis: The process of numerically analyzing the effect on overall project objectives of identified risks.

Regulation: Requirements imposed by a government body. These requirements can establish product, process or service characteristics, including applicable administrative provisions, that have government-mandated compliance.

Reimbursable expenses: Undefined costs that are expended up to a fee not to exceed the amount specified in the RFP and contract.

Reliability: The probability of a product performing its intended function under specific conditions for a given period of time.

Remaining duration (RD): The time in calendar units between the data date of the project schedule and the finish date of the schedule activity that has an actual start date. This represents the time needed to complete a schedule activity that has an actual start date and the time needed to complete a schedule activity where the work is in progress.

Requested change: A formally documented change request that is submitted for approval to the integrated change control process. Contrast with *approved change request*.

Request for information (RFI): A type of procurement document whereby the buyer requests a potential seller to provide various pieces of information related to a product or service, or seller capability.

Request for proposal (RFP): A type of procurement document used to request proposals from prospective sellers of products or services. In some application areas, it may have a narrower or more specific meaning.

Request for quotation (RFQ): A type of procurement document used to request price quotations from prospective sellers of common or standard products or services. Sometimes used in place of a request for proposal, and in some application areas it may have a narrower or more specific meaning.

Request for tender: RFTs are used in conjunction with a contract for construction. Similar to a PCO, it is generated based on the direction of an RFI response.

Requirement: A condition or capability that must be met or possessed by a system, product, service, result, or component to satisfy a contract, standard, specification, or other formally imposed documents. Requirements include the quantified and documented needs, wants, and expectations of the sponsor, customer, and other stakeholders.

Requirements contract: This type of contract allows for goods or services to be supplied exclusively from one supplier, based on a defined amount of time.

Research and development projects (R&D): This is work that an organization does not rely on to keep its operations, but represents work done on a perpetual basis to increase the organization's knowledge in its specific industry to find new applications for a product or service.

Reserve: A provision in the project management plan to mitigate cost and/or schedule risk. Often used with a modifier (e.g., management reserve, contingency reserve) to provide further details on what types of risk are meant to be mitigated. The specific meaning of the modified term varies by application area.

Reserve analysis: An analytical technique to determine the essential features and relationships of components in the project management plan to establish a reserve for the schedule duration, budget, estimated cost, or fund for a project.

Residual risk: A risk that remains after risk responses have been implemented.

Resource breakdown structure (RBS): A hierarchical structure of resources by resource category and resource type, used in resource-leveling schedules and to develop resource-limited schedules, and which may be used to identify and analyze project human resource assignments.

Resource calendar: A calendar of working days and nonworking days that determines those dates on which each specific resource is idle or can be active. Typically defines resource-specific holidays and resource availability periods. See also *project calendar.*

Resource histogram: A bar chart showing the amount of time that a resource is scheduled to work over a series of time periods. Resource availability may be depicted as a line for comparison purposes. Contrasting bars may show the actual amount of resources used as the project progresses.

Resource leveling: Any form of schedule network analysis in which scheduling decisions (start and finish dates) are driven by resource constraints (e.g., limited resource availability or difficult-to-manage changes in resource availability levels).

Resource-limited schedule: A project schedule whose schedule activity, scheduled start dates and scheduled finish dates reflect expected resource availability. A resource-limited schedule does not have any early or late start or finish dates. The resource-limited schedule total float is determined by calculating the difference between the critical path method late finish date and the resource-limited scheduled finish date. Sometimes called resource-constrained schedule. See also *resource leveling*.

Resource planning: See *activity resource estimating*.

Retainage: A portion of a contract payment that is withheld until contract completion to ensure full performance of the contract terms.

Return on investment (ROI): This allows an organization to calculate and predict, with some certainty, the amount of profit it would make on a certain investment.

Rework: Action taken to bring a defective or nonconforming component into compliance with requirements or specifications.

Risk: An uncertain event or condition that, if it occurs, has a positive or negative effect on a project's objectives. See also *risk category* and *risk breakdown structure*.

Risk avoidance: A risk response planning technique for a threat that creates changes to the project management plan, which is meant to either eliminate the risk or to protect the project objectives from its impact. Generally, risk avoidance involves relaxing the time, cost, scope, or quality objectives.

Risk breakdown structure (RBS): A hierarchically organized depiction of the identified project risks arranged by risk category and subcategory that identifies the various areas and causes of potential risks. The risk breakdown structure is often tailored to specific project types.

Risk category: A group of potential causes of risk. Risk causes may be grouped into categories such as technical, external, organizational, environmental, or project management. A category may include subcategories such as technical maturity, weather, or aggressive estimating. See also *risk breakdown structure*.

Risk database: A repository that provides for collection, maintenance, and analysis of data gathered and used in the risk management processes.

Risk identification: The process of determining which risks might affect the project, and documenting their characteristics.

Risk management plan: Document describing how project risk management will be structured and performed on the project. It is contained in or is a subsidiary plan of the project management plan. The risk management plan can be informal and broadly framed, or formal and highly detailed, based on the needs of the project. Information in the risk management plan varies by application area and project size. The risk management plan is different from the risk register that contains the list of project risks, the results of risk analysis, and the risk responses.

Risk mitigation: A risk response planning technique associated with threats that seek to reduce the probability of occurrence or impact of a risk to below an acceptable threshold.

Risk register: The document containing the results of the qualitative risk analysis, quantitative risk analysis, and risk response planning. The risk register details all identified risks, including description, category, cause, probability of occurring, impact(s) on objectives, proposed responses, owners, and current status. The risk register is a component of the project management plan.

Risk response planning: The process of developing options and actions to enhance opportunities and to reduce threats to project objectives.

Risk transference: A risk response planning technique that shifts the impact of the threat to a third party, together with ownership of the response.

Role: A defined function to be performed by a project team member, such as testing, filing, inspecting, and coding.

Rolling wave planning: A form of progressive elaboration planning where the work to be accomplished in the near term is planned in detail at a low level of the work breakdown structure, while the work far in the future is planned at a relatively high level of the work breakdown structure, but the detailed planning of the work to be performed within another one or two periods in the near future is done as work is being completed during the current period.

Root cause analysis: An analytical technique used to determine the basic underlying reason that causes a variance or a defect or a risk. A root cause may be responsible for more than one variance, defect, or risk.

Rough order of magnitude estimate (ROM): Used early on in the project conceptual phase, it has a very broad error range.

Schedule: See *project schedule* and *schedule model.*

Schedule activity: Also called a task, this is a discrete scheduled component of work performed during the course of a project. A schedule activity normally has an estimated duration, an estimated cost, and estimated resource requirement. Schedule activities are connected to other schedule activities or schedule milestones with logical relationships, and are decomposed from work packages.

Schedule control: The process of controlling changes to the project schedule.

Schedule development: The process of analyzing schedule activity sequences, schedule activity durations, resource requirements, and schedule constraints, to create the project schedule.

Scheduled finish date (SF): The point in time that work was scheduled to finish on a schedule activity. The scheduled finish date is normally within the range of dates delineated by the early finish date and the late finish date. It may reflect resource leveling of scarce resources. Sometimes called planned finish date.

Scheduled start date (SS): The point in time that work was scheduled to start on a schedule activity. The scheduled start date is normally within the range of dates delimited by the early start date and the late start date. It may reflect resource leveling of scarce resources. Sometimes called planned start date.

Schedule management plan: The document that establishes criteria and the activities for developing and controlling the project schedule. It is contained in, or is a subsidiary plan of, the project management plan. The schedule management plan may be formal or informal, highly detailed or broadly framed, based on the needs of the project.

Schedule milestone: A significant event in the project schedule, such as an event restraining future work or marking the completion of a major deliverable. A schedule milestone has zero duration. Sometimes called a milestone activity. See also *milestone.*

Schedule model: A model used in conjunction with manual methods or project management software to perform schedule network analysis to generate the project schedule for use in managing the execution of a project. See also *project schedule.*

Schedule network analysis: A technique to identify early and late start dates, as well as early and late finish dates, for the uncompleted portion of project schedule activities. See also *critical path method, critical chain method, what-if analysis,* and *resource leveling.*

Schedule of deliverables (SOD): Outlines the tasks and activities broken down into work packages so that payment milestones can be established.

Schedule performance index (SPI): A measure of schedule efficiency on a project. It is the ratio of earned value (EV) to planned value (PV). SPI = EV ÷ PV. An SPI equal to or greater than 1 indicates a favorable condition and a value of less than 1 indicates an unfavorable condition.

Schedule of values (SOV): Developed by the contractor, it is used by the construction inspector as a basis for payment of work completed.

Schedule variance (SV): A measure of schedule performance on a project. It is the algebraic difference between the earned value (EV) and the planned value (PV). SV = EV − PV.

Schematic design: The starting point for a task order or RFP, it is used so that design firms can perform preliminary layouts for review and approval. A program may or may not be proved, thus requiring the design firm to identify a recommended program as part of this design stage.

Scope: The sum of the products, services, and results to be provided as a project. See also *project scope* and *product scope.*

Scope baseline: See *baseline.*

Scope change: Any change to the project scope. A scope change almost always requires an adjustment to the project cost or schedule.

Scope control: The process of controlling changes to the project scope.

Scope creep: Adding features and functionality (project scope) without addressing the effects on time, costs, and resources, or without customer approval.

Scope definition: The process of developing a detailed project scope statement as the basis for future project decisions.

Scope verification: The process of formalizing acceptance of the completed project deliverables.

S-curve: A graphic display of cumulative costs, labor hours, percentage of work, or other quantities, plotted against time. It is a tool used in quantitative risk analysis used to show a project's PV, EV, and AC.

Secondary risk: A risk that arises as a direct result of implementing a risk response.

Select sellers: The process of reviewing offers, choosing from among potential sellers, and negotiating a written contract with a seller, i.e., a contractor.

Seller: A provider or supplier of products, services, or results to an organization, i.e., a contractor.

Sensitivity analysis: A quantitative risk analysis and modeling technique used to help determine which risks have the most potential impact on the project. It examines the extent to which the uncertainty of each project element affects the objective being examined when all other uncertain elements are held at their baseline values. The typical display of results is in the form of a tornado diagram.

Sepias: Blue prints (blue-lines) developed by the diazo process; an older method of reproducing drawings using a chemical process.

Service: Useful work performed that does not produce a tangible product or result, such as performing any of the business functions supporting production or distribution. Contrast with product and result. See also *deliverable.*

Should-cost estimate: An estimate of the cost of a product or service used to provide an assessment of the reasonableness of a prospective seller's proposed costs.

Simulation: Using a project model that translates the uncertainties specified at a detailed level into their potential impact on objectives that are expressed at the level of the total project. Project simulations use computer models and estimates for risk, usually expressed as a probability distribution of possible costs or durations at a detailed work level, and are typically performed using Monte Carlo analysis.

Six Sigma: A process that helps identify and remove defects and minimize anomalies in product production and in business processes.

Skill: Ability to use knowledge, a developed aptitude, and/or a capability to effectively and readily execute or perform an activity.

Slack: See *total float* and *free float.*

Slack time: Lag time, i.e., float between the start and finish of tasks not on the critical path.

Smart growth: A philosophy of providing designs that are advantageous to the environment and incorporating green design practices into a project.

Soil conservation service: A review agency that approves proposed soil conservation methods to be employed on a project.

Space study: Study requested by an organization when a project program needs developed; a design firm will prepare and submit a proposed program identifying required spaces.

Special cause: A source of variation that is not inherent in the system, is not predictable, and is intermittent. It can be assigned to a defect in the system. On a control chart, points beyond the control limits, or non-random patterns within the control limits, indicate this. Also referred to as assignable cause.

Specification: A document that specifies, in a complete, precise, verifiable manner, the requirements, design, behavior, or other characteristics of a system component, product, result, or service and, often, the procedures for determining whether these provisions have been satisfied. Examples are requirement specifications, design specifications, product specifications, and test specifications.

Specifications limits: The area, on either side of the centerline, or mean, of data plotted on a control chart that meets the customer's requirements for a product or service. These may be greater than or less than the area defined by the control limits. See also *control limits.*

Sponsor: The person or group that provides the financial resources, in cash or in kind, for the project.

Staffing management plan: The document that describes when and how human resource requirements will be met. It is contained in, or is a subsidiary plan of, the project management plan. The staffing management plan can be informal and broadly framed, or formal and highly detailed, based on the need of the project. Information in the staffing management plan varies by application area and project size.

Staff-level review: Approval is required only at the staff level rather than the planning commission approval level. Used mostly during resubmissions of revised site plans.

Stakeholder: Person or organization (e.g., customer, sponsor, performing organizations, user, or the public) that is actively involved in the project, or whose interests may be positively or negatively affected by execution or completion of the project. A stakeholder may also exert influence over the project and its deliverables.

Standard: A document established by consensus and approved by a recognized body that provides, for common and repeated use, rules, guidelines or characteristics for activities or their results, aimed at the achievement of the optimum degree of order in the given context.

Standard operating procedures (SOP): Provides direction to staff on how to perform tasks based on approved organizational methods.

Start date: A point in time associated with a schedule activity's start, usually qualified by one of the following: actual, planned, estimated, scheduled, early, late, target, baseline, or current.

Start-to-finish (SF): The logical relationship where completion of the successor schedule activity is dependent upon the initiation of the predecessor schedule activity. See also *logical relationship.*

Start-to-start (SS): The logical relationship where initiation of the work of the successor schedule activity depends upon the initiation of the work of the predecessor schedule activity. See also *logical relationship.*

Statement of qualifications (SOQ): Documents developed by organizations to provide directions and project details to interested design firms.

Statement of work (SOW): A narrative description of products, services, or results to be supplied.

Stormwater management design: Provided by the design firm's civil engineer, it provides a design that addresses mitigation measures used to control and/or treat stormwater.

Strengths, weaknesses, opportunities, and threats (SWOT) analysis: This information-gathering technique examines the project from the perspective of each project's strengths, weaknesses, opportunities, and threats to increase the breadth of the risks considered by risk management.

Subject matter experts (SMEs): persons providing a specific job, expertise, or specialty service that an organization may not have in-house.

Submittal log: Tracks status of submittals, providing a composite of approved, submitted, and rejected submittals.

Subnetwork: A subdivision (fragment) of a project schedule network diagram, usually representing a subproject or a work package. Often used to illustrate or study some potential or proposed schedule condition, such as changes in preferential schedule logic or project scope.

Subproject: A smaller portion of the overall project created when a project is subdivided into more manageable components or pieces. A subproject is usually represented in the work breakdown structure. A subproject can be referred to as a project, managed as a project and acquired from a seller, and may be referred to as a subnetwork in a project schedule network diagram.

Substantial completion: A construction document indicting that major work has been completed and use and occupancy achieved, thus allowing operation of the product for its intended use.

Successor: See *successor activity.*

Successor activity/task: A group of related schedule activities aggregated at some summary level, and displayed/reported as a single activity at that summary level. See also *subproject* and *subnetwork.*

Sundries: Miscellaneous items too small, and of too little value, to be individually listed.

Sunk cost: Unrecoverable funds required to pay for initial costs of a project.

System: An integrated set of regularly interacting or interdependent components created to accomplish a defined objective, with defined and maintained relationships among its components.

Target completion date (TC): An imposed date that constrains or otherwise modifies the schedule network analysis.

Target finish date (TF): The date that work is planned (targeted) to finish on a schedule activity.

Target schedule: A schedule adopted for comparison purposes during schedule network analysis, which can be different from the baseline schedule. See also *baseline.*

Target start date (TS): The date that work is planned (targeted) to start on a schedule activity.

Task: A term for work whose meaning and placement within a structured plan for project work varies by the application areas, industry, and brand of project management software.

Task order contract: A document used after an IDQ is awarded, it allows a firm to provide a fee proposal for work based on a SOW within a given period of time. Once reviewed and approved, the firm will sign a task order contract with the organization, thus authorizing the work.

Task order: Used in conjunction with an IDQ, it allows PMs to request fee proposals for work that does not require the effort of an RFP process.

Team members: See *project team members.*

Technical performance measurement: A performance measurement technique that compares technical accomplishments during project execution to the project management plan's schedule of planned technical achievements. It may use key technical parameters of the product produced by the project as a quality metric. The achieved metric values are part of the work performance information.

Technique: A defined systematic procedure employed by a human resource to perform an activity to produce a product or result or deliver a service, and that may employ one or more tools.

Template: A partially complete document in a predefined format that provides a defined structure for collecting, organizing, and presenting information and data. Templates are often based upon documents created during prior projects. Templates can reduce the effort needed to perform work and increase the consistency of results. Templates are also called boilerplate documents.

Threat: A condition or situation unfavorable to the project, a negative set of circumstances, a negative set of events, a risk that will have a negative impact on a project objective if it occurs, or a possibility for negative changes. Contrast with *opportunity*.

Three-point estimate: An analytical technique that uses three cost or duration estimates to represent the optimistic, most likely, and pessimistic scenarios. This technique is applied to improve the accuracy of the estimates of cost or duration when the underlying activity or cost component is uncertain. Also is similar to the PERT method.

Threshold: A cost, time, quality, technical, or resource value used as a parameter, and which may be included in the product specifications. Crossing the threshold should trigger some action, such as generating an exception report.

Time and material (T&M) contract: A type of contract that is a hybrid contractual arrangement containing aspects of both cost-reimbursable and fixed-price contracts. Time and material contracts resemble cost-reimbursable type arrangements in that they have no definitive end, because the full value of the arrangement is not defined at the time of the award. Thus, time and material contracts can grow in contract value as if they were cost-reimbursable-type arrangements. Conversely, time and material arrangements can also resemble fixed-price arrangements. For example, the unit rates are present by the buyer and seller, when both parties agree on the rates for the category of senior engineers.

Time-now date: See *data date*.

Time-scaled schedule network diagram: Any project schedule network diagram drawn in such a way that the positioning and length of the schedule activity represents its duration. Essentially, it is a bar chart that includes schedule network logic.

Time value of money: The value of money based on providing a given amount of interest earned over a given amount of time.

Tool: Something tangible, such as a template or software program, used in performing an activity to produce a product or result.

Total float: The total amount of time that a schedule activity may be delayed from its early start date without delaying the project finish date, or violating a schedule constraint. It is calculated using the critical path method technique and determining the difference between the early finish dates and late finish dates. See also *free float.*

Total quality management (TQM): A common approach to implementing a quality improvement program within an organization.

Trend analysis: An analytical technique that uses mathematical models to forecast future outcomes based on historical results. It is a method of determining the variance from a baseline of a budget, cost, schedule, or scope parameter by using prior progress reporting periods' data and projecting how much that parameter's variance from baseline might be at some future point in the project, if no changes are made in executing the project.

Triggers: Indications that a risk has occurred or is about to occur. Triggers may be discovered in the risk identification process and watched in the risk monitoring and control process. Triggers are sometimes called risk symptoms or warning signs.

Triple constraint: A framework for evaluating competing demands. The triple constraint is often depicted as a triangle where one of the sides or corners represents one of the parameters being managed by the project team: cost, schedule (i.e., time), and scope/quality. A PM must keep all three in balance in order to meet organizational goals.

Unforeseen conditions change order: Produced when an item not anticipated in a project is discovered during construction and is required in order to complete the project.

Use and occupancy (U&O): Allows the organization user agency to occupy and operate a facility after substantial completion.

User: The person or organization that will use the project's product or service. See also *customer.*

User requested change order: Requested by the organization's user agency, it is work not defined during design but requested during construction, and would not be required to complete the project as designed.

Value engineering (VE): A creative approach used to optimize project life cycle costs, save time, increase profits, improve quality, expand market share, solve problems, and/or use resources more effectively.

Variance: A quantifiable deviation, departure, or divergence away from a known baseline or expected value.

Variance analysis: A method for resolving the total variance in the set of scope, cost, and schedule variables into specific component variances that are associated with defined factors affecting these variables.

Verification: The technique of evaluating a component or product at the end of a phase or project to assure or confirm it satisfies the conditions imposed.

Virtual team: A group of persons with a shared objective who fulfill their roles with little or no time spent meeting face to face. Various forms of technology are often used to facilitate communication among team members. Virtual teams can be comprised of persons separated by great distances.

Voice of the customer: A planning technique used to provide products, services, and results that truly reflect customer requirements, by translating those requirements into the appropriate technical requirements for each phase of project product development.

War room: A room used for project conferences and planning, often displaying charts of cost, schedule status, and other key project data.

What-if analysis: A simulation technique that allows the PM to identify alternative options in the schedule model.

Work: Sustained physical or mental effort, exertion, or exercise of skill to overcome obstacles and achieve an objective.

Workaround: A response to negative risk that has occurred. It is distinguished from a contingency plan in that a workaround is not planned in advance of the occurrence of the risk event.

Work authorization: A permission and direction, typically written, to begin work on a specific schedule activity or work package or control account. It is a method for sectioning project work to ensure that the work is done by the identified organization, at the right time, and in the proper sequence.

Work authorization system: A subsystem of the overall project management system. It is a collection of formal documented procedures that define how project work will be authorized (committed) to ensure that the work is done by the identified organization, at the right time, and in the proper sequence. It includes the steps, documents, tracking system, and defined approval levels needed to issue work authorizations.

Work breakdown structure (WBS): A deliverable-oriented hierarchical decomposition of the work to be executed by the project team to accomplish the project objectives and create the required deliverables. The WBS organizes and defines the total scope of the project. Each descending level represents an increasingly detailed definition of the project work. The WBS is decomposed into work packages and more manageable chunks. The deliverable orientation of the hierarchy includes both internal and external deliverables. See also *control account*.

Work breakdown structure component: An entry in the work breakdown structure that can be at any level.

Work breakdown structure dictionary: A document that describes each component in the work breakdown structure (WBS). For each WBS component, the WBS dictionary includes a brief definition of the scope or statement of work, defined deliverable(s), a list of associated activities, and a list of milestones. Other information may include responsible organizations, start and end dates, resources required, and estimate of cost, charge number, contract information, quality requirements, and technical references to facilitate performance of the work.

Work item: Term no longer in common usage. See *activity* and *schedule activity*.

Work performance information: Information and date on the status of the project schedule activities being performed to accomplish the project work, collected as part of the direct and manage project execution processes. Information includes status of deliverables; implementation status for change requests, corrective actions, preventive actions, and defect repairs; forecasted estimates to complete; reported percent of work physically completed; achieved value of technical performance measures; and start and finish dates of schedule activities.

Zoning regulations: Rules when developing land that requires infrastructural components before any other development can take place.

Abbreviations

AC	Actual cost
ACSM	American Congress on Surveying and Mapping
ACWP	Actual cost of work performed
AD	Activity description
A/E	Architect/engineer
AEC	Architecture, engineering, and construction industry
ALTA	American Land Title Association
ANSI	American National Standards Institute
AOA	Activity on arrow
AON	Activity on node
APFO	Adequate public facilities ordinance
BAC	Budget at completion
BCWP	Budgeted cost of work performed
BCWS	Budgeted cost of work scheduled
BOCC	Board of county commissioners
BOD	Basis of design
CA	Construction administration services
CBA	Cost-benefit analysis
CCD	Construction change directive
CDs	Construction drawing documents
CIP	Capital improvement program
CM	Construction manager
CPF	Cost-plus-fee contract
CPFF	Cost-plus-fixed fee contract
CPI	Cost performance index
CPIF	Cost-plus-incentive fee contract

CPM	Critical path method
CPPC	Cost-plus-percentage of cost contract
CSC	Consultant selection committee
CSI	Construction Specifications Institute
CV	Cost variance
DCMI	Department of construction management and inspection
DD	Data date
DDs	Design development documents
DQC	Definite quantity contract
EAC	Estimate at completion
ECS	Environmental compliance section
EF	Early finish
EIFS	Exterior insulation and finishing system
ES	Early start
ESD	Environmental site design
ETC	Estimate to complete
EV	Earned value
EVT	Earned value technique
FF	Finish-to-finish or free float
FFP	Firm-fixed-price contract
FPIF	Firm-price-incentive-fee contract
FRO	Forest resource ordinance
FS	Finish-to-start
FV	Future value
GC	General contractor
GO	General obligation bonds
HVAC	Heating, ventilation, and air conditioning
IDQ	Indefinite quantity contract
IFB	Invitation for bid
IIT	Interagency information technologies department
IPs	Improvement plans
IRR	Internal rate of return
ITB	Invitation to bid
LF	Late finish
LOE	Level of effort
LS	Late start
NOI	Notice of intent
NPDES	National pollution discharge system
NPV	Net present value
O&M	Operations and maintenance manual

OD	Original duration
OPR	Owners project requirements
PC/PTC	Percent complete
PCB	Polychlorinated biphenyls
PCO	Proposed change order
PDM	Precedence diagramming method
PERT	Program evaluation and review technique
PF	Planned finish date
PM	Project manager or project management
PMBOK®	*Project Management Body of Knowledge*, 3rd edition
PMI®	Project Management Institute
PMO	Project management office
PMP®	Project management professional
PO	Purchase order
PS	Planned start date
PV	Planned value or present value
QA	Quality assurance
QBS	Qualifications-based selection
R&D	Research and development
RBS	Resource breakdown structure or risk breakdown structure
RD	Remaining duration
RFI	Request for information
RFP	Request for proposal
RFQ	Request for quote
RFT	Request for tender
ROI	Return on investment
ROM	Rough order of magnitude estimate
SCD	Soil conservation district
SD	Start date
SF	Schedule finish date or start-to-finish
SME	Subject matter expert
SOD	Schedule of deliverables
SOP	Standard operating procedures
SOQ	Statement of qualification
SOV	Schedule of values
SOW	Statement of work
SPI	Schedule performance index
SS	Schedule start date or start-to-start
SV	Schedule variance
SWM	Stormwater management

SWOT	Strengths, weaknesses, opportunities, and threats analysis
T&M	Time and material contract
TC	Target completion date
TCPI	To complete performance index
TF	Target finish date or total float
TQM	Total quality management
TS	Target start date
U&O	Use and occupancy
VAC	Variance at completion
VCT	Vinyl composite tile
VE	Value engineering
WBS	Work breakdown structure

Useful Project Management Formulas

$PV = FV \div (1 + r)^n$

$FV = PV \times (1 + r)^n$

$BCR = \text{Benefit} \div \text{Cost}$

$PERT = (P + 4M + O) \div 6$

$1\,\sigma = 68.26\%$

$2\,\sigma = 95.46\%$

$3\,\sigma = 99.73\%$

$6\,\sigma = 99.99\%$

Control limits are to be within $\pm\,3\,\sigma$ from the mean

Standard deviation $= (P - O) \div 6$

Variance $= [(P - O) \div 6]^2$

Float/slack $= LS - ES$ and $LF - EF$

Cost variance $= EV - AC$

Schedule variance = EV − PV

CPI = EV ÷ AC

SPI = EV ÷ PV

EAC = BAC ÷ CPI

EAC if initial estimates are flawed = AC + ETC

EAC if FVs are not typical = AC + BAC − EV

EAC if FVs are typical = AC + (BAC − EV) ÷ CPI

ETC = EAC − AC

Percent complete = EV ÷ BAC

TCPI = (VAC − EV) ÷ (BAC − AC)

Communication channels = Number of participants × (n − 1) ÷ 2

Forward pass:

- ES = EF of the predecessor

- EF = ES + duration

Backward pass:

- LF = LS of the successor

- LS = LF − duration

Slack = LF − EF = LS − ES

Free Float − ES (successor activity) − EF (predecessor activity)

Index

AC (actual cost). *See* actual cost of work performed

acceptance, 138–39, 155

activity, 7, 155; duration, 20, 58–59, 156; identifier, 20, 156; list, 59, 61, 156; near-critical, 20, 168–69; predecessor, 54, 56, 172; schedule, 5, 20, 180; sequencing, 20, 54, 156; successor, 54, 56, 185

activity on arrow (AOA). *See* arrow diagramming method

activity on node (AON). *See* schedule network

actual cost of work performed (ACWP), 24, 131, 132–33, 156

addendum, 109, 112, 113, 156

adequate public facilities ordinance (APFO), 31, 156

advertisement: construction, 111; SOQ, 37–39, *38*

A/E. *See* architect/engineer

after-action report, 139, *140–45*

allowance, 68, 82–83

ALTA Survey, 147, 156

amendment, budget, 121–22, 158

American Land Title Association Survey. *See* ALTA Survey

analogous estimate, 30, 156–57

analysis: cost-benefit, 9–10, 160; Monte Carlo, 15–16, 168; reserve, 17, 178; risk, 6, 176, 177; root cause, 20, 180; sensitivity, 6, 182; SWOT, 6, 184

AOA (activity on arrow). *See* arrow diagramming method

AON (activity on node). *See* schedule network

APFO. *See* adequate public facilities ordinance

application area, 7, 157

approved change request, 188

architect/engineer (A/E), 21–23, *141–42*

architectural service, 76, 101–7

archive, 137, 145–48

area, application, 7, 157

arrow diagramming method, 54, 157. *See also* schedule network

as-built, 21; drawings, 30, 33, 137–38

attribute, activity, 7, 155

award recommendation, 116, *117–20*

BAC. *See* budget at completion

backflow prevention (BFP), 95, 106

backward pass, 54, 56, 157. *See also* schedule network

balancing change order, 128–29, 157

bar chart, 54, *55*, 157, 166

FFP. *See* firm fixed-price contract
field report, 20, 164
50% construction document. *See* construction document
finish date, 20, 164; early, 54, 162; late, 54, 167; scheduled, 181; target, 185
finish-to-finish (FF), 20, 164. *See also* schedule network
finish-to-start (FS), 20, 164. *See also* schedule network
fire department connection (FDC), 95
firm fixed-price contract (FFP), 23, 165
fixed-price contract, 23–25, 165
fixed-price-incentive-fee contract (FPIF), 23, 165
fixed-price redetermination contract, 24, 165
fixed-price with economic price adjustment contract, 23–24, 165
float: free, 20, 54, 56, 165; total, 20, 186
forest resource ordinance (FRO), 31, 165
forward pass, 54, 56, 165. *See also* schedule network
FPIF. *See* fixed-price-incentive-fee contract
free float (FF), 20, 54, 56, 165
FRO. *See* forest resource ordinance
front end document, 109–10, 165
FS. *See* finish-to-start
functional manager, 12, 165
functional organization, 12, 165
funds. *See* budget
future value (FV), 11, *12*, 165

Gannt chart, 54, *55*, 157, 166
general contractor (GC), 23, 166
general obligation (GO) bond, 10, 166
geotechnical service, 53, 82
GO bond. *See* general obligation bond
go/no-go decision, 10, 166
A Guide to the Project Management Body of Knowledge (*PMBOK Guide*) (Project Management Institute), 5–7, 22, 29–30, 174

hand-off, 121–24
Hanley, Nick, 9–10
hardware (HW), 104
hazardous material, 112
heating, ventilation, and air conditioning (HVAC) system, 18–19, 86, 92, 99, 105–6
HVAC system. *See* heating, ventilation, and air conditioning system
HW. *See* hardware

identifier, activity, 20, 156
IDQ. *See* indefinite quantity contract
IFB. *See* invitation for bid
IIT. *See* interagency information technology
improvement plan (IP), 33, 166
improvement program, capital. *See* capital improvement program
indefinite quantity contract (IDQ), 17–18, 25–28, 35–36, 166
initiating process, 6, 166
inspection, 21, 122–23, 133–35, 166; building, 33, 158; construction, 23, 135, 159; costs, *141*; safety, 33, 87, 99–100, 105
interagency information technology (IIT), 21, 23, 92, 121–23
interdisciplinary coordination, 108–9
internal rate of return (IRR), 11, *12*, 166
interviewer/evaluator, 22, 68, 166; RFP and, 22, 51–52, 61, 66; short list and, 45–47, 66–67; SOQ and, 35–37, 38–39
invitation for bid (IFB), 111, 113–15, 166
IP. *See* improvement plan
IRR. *See* internal rate of return
ITB (invitation to bid). *See* invitation for bid

Kaizen approach, 139, 166
keying meeting, 77, 85, 94
kick-off meeting, 76, 88–89, 167

68-95-99.7 rule, 58–59, *60*, 155
slack, 20, 54, 56, 182. *See also* total
   float
smart growth, 32, 183
SME. *See* subject matter expert
SOD. *See* schedule of deliverables
soil conservation service, 33, 125, 183
SOP. *See* standard operating procedures
SOQ. *See* statement of qualifications
SOV. *See* schedule of values
SOW. *See* statement of work
space study, 28, 183
Spash, Clive L., 9–10
specification, 5, 59, 100, 183
SPI. *See* schedule performance index
sponsor, 15–16, 183
SS. *See* scheduled start date; start-to-
   start
staff-level review, 8–9, 183
stakeholder, 15–16, 116, 148, 183
standard, 100, 107, 183–84; building,
   85; deviation, 58–59, *60*
standard operating procedures (SOP),
   19, 28, 85, 184
start date, 20, 184; early, 54, 162; late,
   54, 167; scheduled, 181; target, 185
start-to-finish (SF), 20, 184
start-to-start (SS), 20, 184
statement of qualifications (SOQ),
   7, 17–18, 22, 184; advertisement,
   37–39, *38*; interviewer/evaluator and,
   35–37, *38–39*; scoring criteria, 39,
   40–44, 44–45
statement of work (SOW), 75–76, 184
stop work directive, 116
stormwater, 32–33, 87–88, 184
strengths, weaknesses, opportunities,
   and threats (SWOT) analysis, 6, 184
structure, breakdown: organization, 62,
   63, 169–70, 175; resource, 16–17,
   178; risk, 6, 179; work, 7, 75–76,
   148, 188
study: feasibility, 27–28, 89, 164; space,
   28, 183

subject matter expert (SME), 7, 58, 184
submittal, 20, 126, 184
subnetwork, 20, 184
subproject, 18, 184
substantial completion, 21, 133–34, 184
successor activity, 54, 56, 185
sundries, 8, 18, 185
sunk cost, 11, 185
SV. *See* schedule variance
SWOT analysis. *See* strengths,
   weaknesses, opportunities, and
   threats analysis

target completion date (TC), 20, 185
target finish date (TF), 20, 185
target start date (TS), 20, 185
task, 1, 22, 26, 185
TC. *See* target completion date
team: design, 20, 162; project, 6, 62, 64,
   176; project management, 29, 175;
   virtual, 12, 187–88
technical performance measurement,
   20, 185
TF. *See* target finish date
35% DD. *See* design development
   document
threat, 6, 184; analysis, 35, 186
three-point estimate, 16–17, 56–57, 186
three-sigma rule, 58–59, *60*, 155
threshold, 20, 186
tie bid, 114–15
time: lag, 20, 54, 56, 167; lead, 20, 53,
   126, 167; time value of money, 11,
   186
time and material (T&M), 24–25, 128, 186
time-now date. *See* data date
T&M. *See* time and material
tool, 12–14, 186
total float, 20, 186
total quality management (TQM), 18,
   176–77, 187
trigger, 20, 187
triple constraint, 6, 99, 139, 187
TS. *See* target start date

unforeseen conditions change order, 116, 121–22, 187
use and occupancy (U&O), 8, 133–34, 139, 187
user, 15–16, 22, 148, 187
user-requested change order, 116, 128–29, 187

VAC. *See* variance at completion
value: earned, 131, 163; earned value management, 129, 131–33; earned value technique, 132–33, 163; future, 11, *12*, 165; net present, 11, *12*, 169; planned, 131, 171; schedule of, 20–21, 126–27, 181; time value of money, 11, 186
value engineering (VE), 137–38, 187
variance, 187; cost, 131–32, 160–61; schedule, 132, 181
variance at completion (VAC), 133
VE. *See* value engineering

verification, 89, 126, 138, 187; safety, 33, 87, 99–100, 105; scope, 20, 182
virtual team, 12, 187–88
voice, of customer, 7, 188

war room, 12, 188
WBS. *See* work breakdown structure
weakness, 6, 184
what-if-analysis, 181, 188
work, 188; actual cost of, 24, 131, 132–33, 156; authorization, 5; rework, 6, 179; statement of, 75–76; stop work directive, 116. *See also* activity; schedule; scope of work
workaround, 6, 128, 148, 189
work breakdown structure (WBS), 7, 75–76, 148, 188

zoning: planning and, 32, 92, 147, 171; regulation, 28, 89–92, 107, 189

About the Author

Kevin P. Vida is a project manager for Frederick County Government in Maryland, has a bachelor of science degree in architectural engineering technology from Fairmont State University, and is a registered project management professional (PMP)®. Having several different jobs in the construction and design industry spanning twenty years of experience, he also owns and occasionally operates a general contracting firm in his spare time with a focus on residential and commercial construction.